Mexican Politics in Transition

Monograph Series, 41
Center for U.S.-Mexican Studies
University of California, San Diego

Mexican Politics in Transition

The Breakdown of a One-Party-Dominant Regime

Wayne A. Cornelius

Center for U.S.-Mexican Studies
University of California, San Diego

THE CENTER FOR U.S.-MEXICAN STUDIES
UNIVERSITY OF CALIFORNIA, SAN DIEGO

Printed in the United States of America

Cover photograph by Francisco Mata Rosas; by permission of Secretaría de Gobernación, Mexico.

ISBN: 1-876367-29-3

Contents

Tables and Figures

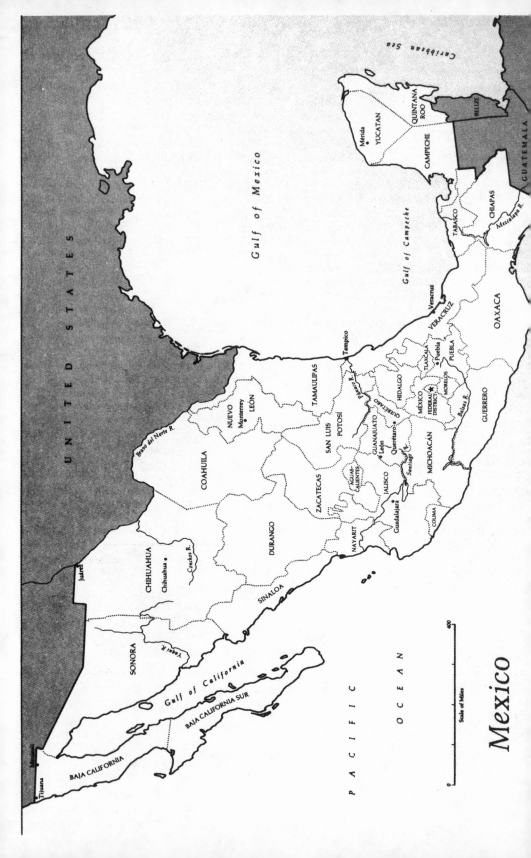

Shattered Illusions:
The Breakdown of a
One-Party-Dominant Regime

On January 1, 1994, Mexico was supposed to be celebrating the beginning of a new era of dynamic, export-led economic growth and prosperity, as the hard-won North American Free Trade Agreement (NAFTA) went into effect. Moreover, Mexico had just become the first developing nation to be permitted to join the Organisation for Economic Co-operation and Development (OECD), the elite organization of the world's most economically advanced countries.

Carlos Salinas de Gortari, generally recognized as Mexico's strongest president since Lázaro Cárdenas in the 1930s, was entering his last year in office, with 70 percent performance approval ratings among the Mexican public and international renown as a successful, free-market economic reformer. Salinas had privatized hundreds of heavily subsidized, inefficient state-owned companies, stabilized the macroeconomy, and slashed inflation from about 160 percent in the year before he took office (1988) to less than 8 percent in 1994. Foreign investment, while below the government's highly optimistic projections, was pouring into the country at an impressive clip. Mexico at last seemed poised to make a giant leap from Third World to First World status.

The ruling Partido Revolucionario Institucional (PRI), in power continuously since 1929, had already nominated its presidential candidate for the August 21 elections. While Salinas would be a tough act to follow for any potential successor, the opposition parties seemed to pose no formidable challenge to continued PRI

The author wishes to thank Jeffrey Weldon, John Bailey, Tomás Calvillo, and Juan Molinar Horcasitas for very helpful suggestions and data which have been incorporated into this monograph.

hegemony and continuity in public policy: divided in their national leadership, weakly grounded in the electorate outside of their regional strongholds, bereft of alternative projects (especially for economic development) that could convincingly deliver results superior to those achieved by the incumbent government, and lacking the "official" party's access to campaign money, mass media attention, and organizing manpower. While political liberalization had proceeded slowly and unevenly under Salinas, far behind the pace of his sweeping economic reforms, Mexico appeared to be coasting inexorably toward a transfer of power to yet another PRI national government.

That illusion of proximate economic modernity and political inevitability was shattered on New Year's Day 1994, by, of all things, a "postmodern" peasant revolt in Chiapas, Mexico's most underdeveloped and politically backward state. An estimated 2,000 primitively armed but well-disciplined Indian rebels seized control of four isolated municipalities and declared war on the central government—something that had not happened since 1938. Their demands for social justice and democracy resonated throughout Mexico, long after the initial skirmishes with the Mexican army had claimed at least 145 lives and a cease-fire had been negotiated. Suddenly, middle- and upper-class Mexicans, as well as foreign governments and investors, were reminded of the persistence of political repression, human rights violations, and extreme poverty and inequality in Mexico, despite all of the progress since 1988 in achieving macroeconomic stability, attracting vast flows of foreign capital, and making the political system more responsive to citizens' concerns. The impoverished Indians who took up arms against the state in Chiapas symbolized the many millions of Mexicans who had been left behind in the drive for economic modernity and internationalism.

The unfinished business of Mexico's free-market economic revolution and the serious social dislocations that it had caused were, indeed, formidable; but they were still considered manageable, within the confines of the one-party-dominant system that had been institutionalized in the 1950s and 1960s. The rebels in Chiapas could be negotiated with and bought off, through a combination of carefully circumscribed political reforms, some land redistribution, and a massive infusion of government funds for social programs and infrastructure. The country could go on to hold national elections in August, installing another PRI president whose policy preferences differed little from those of his two predecessors, thereby locking in Mexico's new, market-driven, internationally "open" economic model.

Masked members of the Zapatista Army of National Liberation (EZLN), led by Subcomandante Marcos (right), meet with government peace negotiators on February 22, 1994. While government troops reoccupied much of the territory seized by the EZLN rebels, several rounds of negotiations failed to resolve the basic conflicts in Chiapas. By late 1995, the stalemate persisted. Source: *Damian Dovarganes/AP/Wide World.*

Those comfortable assumptions were soon to be shattered as well. Less than three months after the Chiapas rebellion erupted, President Salinas's handpicked successor, Luis Donaldo Colosio, was assassinated while campaigning in Tijuana, probably by conservative members of his own party. Colosio had launched his bid for the presidency with bold promises to accelerate the pace of political reform. Apart from raising the specter of uncontrolled political violence and an economy deflated by massive capital flight, Colosio's assassination—the first killing of a national-level political leader in Mexico since 1929—totally disrupted the traditional presidential succession process and reopened divisions within the national political elite that, as recently as 1988, had threatened to split the ruling party.

As in 1988, the fire was put out—but only temporarily. With a last great exertion of presidential will, Carlos Salinas was able to impose upon the PRI another handpicked successor, economist-technocrat Ernesto Zedillo Ponce de León, to replace the slain Colosio. Rapid, skillful responses by Salinas's economic cabinet, strongly backed by the U.S. government, proved sufficient to calm the financial markets. The upsurge in political and drug-related violence that marked 1994 in Mexico even handed the ruling party a potent new issue that it could exploit in the national electoral campaign. Appealing once again to the Mexican public's innate conservatism and fear of violence, the PRI could portray itself as the ultimate guarantor of political stability and nonviolent social change, while frightening voters with visions of the economic and political chaos that would supposedly follow an opposition take-over of the federal government.

The opposition parties to the right and left of the PRI were soundly defeated, in a high-turnout election that was judged by most independent observers to be the cleanest in Mexico's post-revolutionary history. Not only did the PRI retain control of the presidency[1] (albeit with just a plurality of 48.8 percent of the total votes cast); it expanded its majority in the federal Congress. The PRI's intellectual critics were stunned, and the principal leftist opposition party—whose presidential candidate finished a poor third—seemed about to implode. The virtual absence of checks and balances in a political system so dominated by the PRI loomed as the principal obstacle to further democratization, as Mexico approached the end of the century.

The illusion of restored stability created by the ruling party's impressive performance in the August elections was short-lived, however. A militarily insignificant renewal of the Zapatista rebels' activities in Chiapas in December 1994, followed immediately by a sustained speculative attack on the overvalued peso by short-term foreign and domestic investors, opened a Pandora's box of economic and political troubles. Exacerbated by the widespread perception of newly inaugurated President Zedillo as an extraordinarily weak and indecisive leader, what began as a currency and

---

[1] According to statistics of the Federal Electoral Institute (IFE), Zedillo won 50.17 percent of the *valid* votes, that is, excluding 1,001,058 "spoiled" ballots and write-in votes cast for unregistered candidates. However, if the calculation is based on *total* votes cast (including those annulled by election authorities), Zedillo's share of the vote declines to 48.76 percent. The latter method of figuring is more politically meaningful, because it includes "protest" votes cast by those who deliberately spoiled their ballots, for example, by voting for all the candidates listed or writing in the name of an unregistered candidate—even a long-dead historical figure.

financial liquidity crisis quickly evolved into a full-blown crisis of confidence in the PRI-dominated regime and its competence to manage the economy. More than $10 billion in investment capital fled Mexico within a week; the peso had to be sharply devalued, eventually losing more than half of its value against the U.S. dollar, and the government came within a few days of insolvency as its foreign currency reserves were depleted. Only a $52 billion international financial bailout action orchestrated by the U.S. government forestalled a complete collapse of the economy. The Zedillo government, desperate to strengthen itself and prevent any additional conflicts of a political nature, began making private deals with the opposition parties, some of which were openly resisted by PRI militants. Ex-President Salinas, who had publicly criticized Zedillo and his economic cabinet for provoking the economic crisis by mishandling the December 1994 devaluation of the peso, was sent by Zedillo into de facto exile in the United States.

Ironically, it was Salinas who had breathed life into the creaking PRI apparatus in the five years following his own disputed election to the presidency. In the July 6, 1988, national elections, the PRI had suffered unprecedented reverses in both the presidential and congressional races. For the first time in history, a Mexican president had been elected with less than half of the votes cast— 48.7 percent, and probably much less, if the vote count had been honest.[2] This was more than 20 percentage points below the vote share attributed to PRI presidential candidate Miguel de la Madrid in the 1982 election. Ex-PRIista Cuauhtémoc Cárdenas, son of the much-revered former President Lázaro Cárdenas, heading a hastily assembled coalition of minor leftist and nationalist parties, was officially credited with 31.1 percent of the presidential vote—far

---

[2]If the 695,042 "spoiled" ballots and 14,333 votes cast for nonregistered presidential candidates in the 1988 election are excluded from the percentage base, Salinas's share rises to a bare majority (50.74 percent). The actual extent of irregularities in the 1988 presidential vote tabulation will never be determined. Within a few hours after the polls closed, a "computer crash" in the National Registry of Voters allegedly interrupted the count, and six days would pass before even preliminary results for a majority of the country's polling places were announced. It was not until 1994 that a knowledgeable election official confirmed the widespread suspicion that there had been no "computer crash" on election night in 1988. In fact, higher authorities ordered the computerized count to be suspended after early returns showed Cárdenas leading by a significant margin. There is no evidence from exit surveys of voters leaving polling places in 1988, because the government had denied permission for such surveys. Nevertheless, the official tally for Salinas was within a few percentage points of his showing in several of the most scientifically reliable preelection polls. (See Miguel Basáñez, "Las encuestas y los resultados oficiales, *Perfil de La Jornada*, August 8, 1988.) Based on detailed analyses of the partial, publicly released election results, most analysts have concluded that Salinas probably did win, but that his margin of victory over Cárdenas was much smaller than the 19-point spread indicated by the official results.

more than any previous opposition candidate. A diminished PRI delegation still controlled the Congress, but the president's party had lost the two-thirds majority needed to approve constitutional amendments.

Salinas's brand of strong presidential leadership and his ac-complishments—especially the sharp reduction in inflation and the implementation of a new-style "antipoverty" and public works program which greatly increased government responsiveness to lower-class demands—sufficed to rebuild electoral support for the PRI and to paper over the cracks within the ruling political class. The widely predicted open rupture of the elite, possibly leading to the PRI's demise and a fully competitive, democratic political system, did not occur during Salinas's presidency.

After the political and economic shocks of 1994, however, the world's longest-ruling political party once again appeared to be in a state of accelerated decomposition. By early 1995 the system of strong presidential rule was threatened by an unprecedented breakdown of discipline within the PRI and a fully resuscitated conservative opposition party, which would take or retain control of four important state governments in elections held during the year.

Apart from the massive loss of national wealth signified by the mega-devaluation and capital flight of 1994–1995, revelations that serious macroeconomic problems and mismanagement had been concealed from the electorate by the Salinas administration during the run-up to the 1994 elections fueled public anger toward the government. Having returned the PRI to power for another six years—in part because they doubted the ability of the opposition parties to run the country's economy as successfully as PRI techno-crats seemingly had done since 1988—Mexicans now faced a long period of negative or anemic economic growth, inflation in the high double-digit range, massive job losses (over 1 million in 1995 alone), sharply increased taxation, austerity budgets, greater financial dependence on the United States, and high political uncertainty.

Middle-class Mexicans, in particular, felt betrayed by a govern-ment that had purchased their electoral loyalty with a flood of imported consumer goods (made affordable by the overvalued peso), readily available consumer credit, and inflated promises of rapid, NAFTA-driven economic growth that would raise incomes and keep everyone employed. Instead, they got a shrinking econ-omy, high employment insecurity, and an unmanageable debt burden, as interest rates for auto loans, home mortgages, and credit card balances soared above 80 percent. The number of overdue loans held by private banks rose so rapidly that the solvency of the entire banking system was threatened, and a nationwide movement of middle-class debtors demanded a government-imposed moratorium on loan repayments.

In 1995, for the first time in memory, prominent Mexican intellectuals, media commentators, and politicians openly began discussing the possibility that an elected PRI president might be unable to finish his term. Zedillo, some predicted, would either be forced to resign by a generalized crisis of credibility and governability, or he would be removed in a coup led by old-guard PRI leaders, perhaps in league with military officers frustrated by the seemingly endless rebellion in Chiapas.[3] Neither of these scenarios, nor what Mexican commentators now refer to as "East Europeanization"—uncontrolled societal mobilization causing an abrupt collapse of the PRI regime—seems probable at this juncture. However, divisions within the ruling coalition are deeper than at any time since the mid-1930s, when newly inaugurated, reform-minded President Lázaro Cárdenas forced a confrontation with long-time strongman and former President Plutarco Elías Calles and his conservative allies. Under present circumstances, a slow-motion implosion of the regime, resembling what happened in the Soviet Union in the late Gorbachev era, cannot be ruled out.

Only a decade ago, such drastic changes in the Mexican political system would have seemed unthinkable. This regime had been the most stable in the modern history of Latin America, with a well-earned reputation for resilience, adaptability to new circumstances, a high level of agreement within the ruling elite on basic rules of political competition, and a high capacity to co-opt dissidents, both within and outside of the ruling party. As late as 1990, the celebrated Peruvian novelist Mario Vargas Llosa could plausibly describe Mexico's regime as "the perfect dictatorship," combining stability, legitimacy, and durability in a way that even the former Soviet Union and Castro's Cuba had never been able to achieve.[4]

Since 1929, when the "official" party was founded, both political assassination and armed rebellion had been rejected as routes to the presidency by all contenders for power. A handful of disappointed aspirants to the ruling party's presidential nomination mounted candidacies outside the party (in the elections of 1929, 1940, 1946, 1952, and 1988), but even the most broadly

---

[3]In a national survey of middle- and upper-income Mexicans, conducted by MORI de México during February 24–27, 1995, nearly half of the respondents agreed that a coup d'état was possible in Mexico, if President Zedillo's handling of the economic and political crisis did not improve; only 38 percent considered such an event impossible (*Este País* [Mexico City] 49 [April 1995], p. 50).

[4]Quoted in Denise Dresser, "Five Scenarios for Mexico," *Journal of Democracy* 5:3 (July 1994), p. 57.

supported of these breakaway movements were successfully contained through government-engineered vote fraud and intimidation.

In the early 1970s concerns had been raised about the stability of the system, after the bloody repression of a student protest movement in Mexico City by President Gustavo Díaz Ordaz on the eve of the 1968 Olympic Games. Many analysts at that time suggested that Mexico was entering a period of institutional crisis, requiring fundamental reforms in both political arrangements and strategy of economic development. But the discovery of massive oil and natural gas resources during the last half of the decade gave the incumbent regime a new lease on life. The continued support of masses and elites could be purchased with an apparently limitless supply of petro-pesos, even without major structural reforms. The government's room for maneuver was abruptly erased by the collapse of the oil boom in August 1982, owing to a combination of adverse international economic circumstances (falling oil prices, rising interest rates, recession in the United States) and fiscally irresponsible domestic policies. Real wages and living standards for the vast majority of Mexicans plummeted, and the government committed itself to a socially painful restructuring of the economy, including a drastic shrinkage of the sector owned and managed by the government itself.

The economic crisis of the 1980s placed enormous stress on Mexico's political system. Indeed, as both Presidents de la Madrid and Salinas argued, the absence of a social explosion throughout the "lost decade" of the 1980s could be taken as evidence of the essential strength of Mexico's political institutions. But the apparent recovery of economic health in the 1989–1993 period did not reverse the decline of the hegemonic one-party regime. The 1988 election results had demonstrated that the political system whose basic elements were put in place by Lázaro Cárdenas in the 1930s had outlived its usefulness. The strong performance of opposition candidates of both right and left in several of the gubernatorial elections held during the Salinas presidency proved that the 1988 national election was no fluke. In 1989 the PRI's 60-year-old monopoly of state governorships was finally broken, with the overwhelming, officially recognized victory of Ernesto Ruffo, candidate of the conservative Partido Acción Nacional (PAN), in Baja California. By May 1995, three additional state governments had been "surrendered" by the PRI to the PAN (in Guanajuato, Chihuahua, and Jalisco). By November 1995, the PAN had made such gains in state and local elections that it governed some 35 million Mexicans— over one-third of the country's population.

These opposition gains, occurring in some of the country's most highly developed states, suggest that Mexican society—increasingly complex, heterogeneous, more urban, better educated, more integrated into the world economy—has simply outgrown the political institutions and patterns of state-society relations largely established in the 1930s. Centralized control of both mass publics and members of the political class has become increasingly difficult to maintain. In 1994, the PRI was miraculously able to pull its feuding factions together sufficiently to win, convincingly, one more national election. But the current economic crisis certainly has the potential to "put an end to the Mexican political system as we know it," as Mexican novelist–political activist Carlos Fuentes has predicted.[5] The main questions now are what set of political structures and arrangements will replace it, and how conflictual the transition process will be.

[5]Quoted in *El Financiero International*, April 3–9, 1995, p. 2.

Historical Perspective

LEGACIES OF COLONIALISM

Long before Hernán Cortés landed in 1519 and began the Spanish conquest of Mexico, its territory was inhabited by numerous Indian civilizations. Of these, the Maya in the Yucatán peninsula and the Toltec on the central plateau had developed the most complex political and economic organization. Both of these civilizations had disintegrated, however, before the Spaniards arrived. Smaller Indian societies were decimated by diseases introduced by the invaders or were vanquished by the sword. Subsequent grants of land and Indian labor by the Spanish Crown to the colonists further isolated the rural Indian population and deepened their exploitation.

The combined effects of attrition, intermarriage, and cultural penetration of Indian regions have drastically reduced the proportion of Mexico's population culturally identified as Indian. By 1990, according to census figures, 7.9 percent of the nation's population spoke an Indian language.[1] The Indian minority has been persistently marginal to the national economy and political system. Today, the indigenous population is heavily concentrated in rural communities that the government classifies as the country's most economically depressed and service-deprived, located primarily in the southeast and the center of the country.[2] They engage in rainfall-dependent subsistence agriculture using traditional methods of cultivation, are seasonally employed as migrant laborers in commercial agriculture, or produce crafts for sale in regional and national markets. The Indian population is an espe-

---

[1] This represents an undercount, since the census identifies as Indians only persons over the age of five. Indians of all ages constitute an estimated 15 percent of the total population.

[2] See Jaime Sepúlveda, ed., *La salud de los pueblos indígenas en México* (México, D.F.: Secretaría de Salud and Instituto Nacional Indigenista, September 1993).

cially troubling reminder of the millions of people who have been left behind by uneven development in twentieth-century Mexico.

The importance of Spain's colonies in the New World lay in their ability to provide the Crown with vital resources to fuel the Spanish economy. Mexico's mines provided gold and silver in abundance until the war of independence began in 1810. After independence, Mexico continued to export these ores, supplemented in subsequent eras by hemp, cotton, textiles, oil, and winter vegetables.

The Crown expected the colony to produce enough basic food crops for its own sustenance. Agriculture developed, unevenly, alongside the resource-exporting sectors of the economy. Some farming was small-scale subsistence agriculture. Most large landholdings in the colonial era were farmed through combinations of sharecropping, debt peonage, and large-scale cultivation; they produced basic food grains and livestock for regional markets. Over the nineteenth century, some large landholders made significant capital investments in machinery to process agricultural products (grain mills and textile factories) and in agricultural inputs (land, dams, and improved livestock). These agricultural entrepreneurs produced commercial crops for the national or international market. Today, the relationship between subsistence agriculture on tiny plots (*minifundia*) and large-scale, highly mechanized commercial agriculture is far more complex; but the extreme dualism and the erratic performance that characterize Mexico's agricultural sector are among the most important bottlenecks in the country's economic development.

CHURCH AND STATE

Since the Spanish conquest, the Roman Catholic Church has been an institution of enduring power in Mexico, but the nature of its power has changed notably in the postcolonial era. Priests joined the Spanish invaders in an evangelical mission to promote conversion of the Indians to Catholicism, and individual priests have continued to play important roles in national history. Father Miguel Hidalgo y Costilla helped launch Mexico's war of independence in 1810, and Father José María Morelos y Pavón replaced Hidalgo as spiritual and military leader of the independence movement when Hidalgo was executed by the Crown in 1811.

During Mexico's postindependence period, institutional antagonisms between church and central government have occasionally flared into open confrontations on such issues as church wealth, educational policy, the content of public school textbooks, and political activism by the church. The constitutions of 1857 and

1917 formally established the separation of church and state and defined their respective domains. Constitutional provisions dramatically reduced the church's power and wealth by nationalizing its property, including large agricultural landholdings. The 1917 constitution also made church-affiliated schools subject to the authority of the federal government, denied priests the right to vote or speak publicly on political issues, and gave the government the right to limit the number of priests who can serve in Mexico.

Government efforts during the 1920s to enforce these constitutional provisions led the church to suspend religious services throughout the country. Church leaders also supported the Cristero rebellion of 1927–1929, as a last stand against the incursions of a centralizing state. Large landholders took advantage of the conflict, inciting devout peasants to take up arms against local dissidents who had begun to petition the government for land reform. Because the church also opposed redistribution of land, the landowners could depict themselves as faithful partners in the holy war against a state that espoused such policies. The rebellion caused 100,000 combatant deaths, uncounted civilian casualties, and economic devastation in a large part of central Mexico. The settlement of the conflict established, once and for all, the church's subordination to the state, in return for which the government relaxed its restrictions on church activities in nonpolitical arenas.

This accord inaugurated a long period of relative tranquility in church-state relations, during which many of the anticlerical provisions of the 1917 constitution (such as the prohibition on church involvement in education) were ignored by both the government and the church. The central church hierarchy—among the most conservative in Latin America—cooperated with the government on a variety of issues, and the church posed no threat to the ruling party's hegemony.

Today, the church retains considerable influence, particularly in Mexico's rural areas and small cities. But even though more than 80 percent of the country's population identify themselves as Catholics in sample surveys, this religious preference does not translate automatically into support for the church's positions on social or political issues. Formal church opposition to birth control, for example, has not prevented widespread adoption of family planning practices in Mexico since the government launched a birth control program in the mid-1970s. Nevertheless, the government respects and perhaps even fears the Catholic Church's capacity for mass mobilization, which was demonstrated dramatically during Pope John Paul II's visits to Mexico in 1979 and 1990. On each of those occasions, an estimated 20 million Mexicans participated in street demonstrations and other public gatherings held in connection with the papal visit. In 1990 a well-organized protest movement organized by the Catholic Church in response to a state law legalizing abortions in the southern state of Chiapas succeeded in overturning the law, virtually ending hopes for liberalizing abortion laws throughout Mexico.

Since the 1980s church-state relations have been strained by the highly visible political activism of some local and state-level church leaders. In the northern state of Chihuahua, for example, the archbishop publicly criticized PRI fraud in the July 1986 gubernatorial election and sided openly with the candidate of the Partido Acción Nacional (PAN). In the southern state of Chiapas during 1994 and 1995, Bishop Samuel Ruiz García served as mediator between the Zapatista rebels and the federal government. Closely identified with the cause of the state's impoverished Indian population, Ruiz was accused by hard-liners within the PRI-government apparatus and even by conservative members of the Catholic Church hierarchy of being a provocateur and Marxist revolutionary who helped to organize the rebellion or, at minimum, knew that it was being planned.

This and other episodes of overt political activism by church leaders and priests have been poorly tolerated by most members of the ruling political elite. But President Carlos Salinas de Gortari, determined to "modernize" church-state relations, induced the Congress to repeal many of the constitutionally mandated restrictions on religious activities (including church-run private schools), while maintaining the prohibition on overt participation of the clergy in partisan politics. In 1992 the Salinas government also resumed diplomatic relations with the Vatican, which had been suspended for 128 years. Opinion polls showed broad public support for these steps toward normalizing church-state relations.[3]

However, the assassination of Juan Jesús Posadas, Cardinal of Guadalajara, in May 1993 opened a major new breach, with the government claiming that the cardinal was the unintended victim of a confrontation between rival drug-trafficking organizations while Posadas's successor contended that he had been deliberately targeted for elimination by groups or persons unknown. The still unsolved assassination case and the involvement of church leaders and laymen in the Chiapas conflict promise to generate continuing tension in the church-state relationship.

REVOLUTION AND ITS AFTERMATH

The civil conflict that erupted in Mexico in 1910 is often referred to as the first of the great "social revolutions" that shook the world early in the twentieth century, but Mexico's upheaval originated

---

[3]See, for example, "Encuestalía: ¿Quién quiere un Papa?" *Nexos* 148 (April 1990).

within the country's ruling class. The revolution did not begin as a spontaneous uprising of the common people against an entrenched dictator, Porfirio Díaz, and against the local bosses and landowners who exploited them. Even though hundreds of thousands of workers and peasants ultimately participated in the civil strife, most of the revolutionary leadership came from the younger generation of middle- and upper-class Mexicans who had become disenchanted with three and a half decades of increasingly heavy-handed rule by the aging dictator and his clique. These disgruntled members of the elite saw their future opportunities for economic and political mobility blocked by the closed group surrounding Díaz.

Led by Francisco I. Madero, whose family had close ties with the ruling group, these liberal bourgeois reformers were committed to opening up the political system and creating new opportunities for themselves within a capitalist economy whose basic features they did not challenge. They sought not to destroy the established order but rather to make it work more in their own interest than that of the foreign capitalists who had come to dominate key sectors of Mexico's economy during the Porfirian dictatorship, a period called "the Porfiriato."

Of course, some serious grievances had accumulated among workers and peasants. Once the rebellion against Díaz got under way, leaders who appealed to the disadvantaged masses pressed their claims against the central government. Emiliano Zapata led a movement of peasants in the state of Morelos who were bent on regaining the land they had lost to the rural aristocracy by subterfuge during the Porfiriato. In the north, Pancho Villa led an army consisting of jobless workers, small landowners, and cattle hands, whose main interest was steady employment. As the various revolutionary leaders contended for control of the central government, the political order that had been created and enforced by Díaz disintegrated into warlordism—powerful regional gangs led by revolutionary *caudillos* (political-military strongmen) who aspired more to increasing their personal wealth and social status than to leading a genuine social revolution. In sum, "although class conflict was central to the Revolution, the Revolution cannot be reduced to class conflict. . . . [It] was a mix of different classes, interests, and ideologies," giving rise to a state that enjoyed considerable autonomy vis-à-vis specific class interests.[4]

The first decade of the revolution produced a new, remarkably progressive constitution, replacing the constitution of 1857. The

---

[4]Alan Knight, "Revolutionary Project, Recalcitrant People: Mexico, 1910–1940," in Jaime E. Rodríguez, ed., *The Revolutionary Process in Mexico* (Los Angeles, Calif.: UCLA Latin American Center, 1990), pp. 228–29.

young, middle-class elite that dominated the constitutional convention of 1916–1917 "had little if any direct interest in labor unions or land distribution. But it was an elite that recognized the need for social change. . . . By 1916, popular demands for land and labor reform were too great to ignore."[5] The constitution of 1917 established the principle of state control over all natural resources, subordination of the church to the state, the government's right to redistribute land, and rights for labor that had not yet been secured even by the labor movement in the United States. Nearly two decades passed, however, before most of these constitutional provisions began to be implemented.

Many historians today stress the continuities between pre-revolutionary and postrevolutionary Mexico. The processes of economic modernization, capital accumulation, state building, and political centralization that gained considerable momentum during the Porfiriato were interrupted by civil strife from 1910 to 1920, but they resumed once a semblance of order had been restored. During the 1920s, the central government set out to eliminate or undermine the most powerful and independent-minded regional *caudillos* by co-opting the local power brokers (known traditionally as *caciques*). These local political bosses became, in effect, appendages of the central government, supporting its policies and maintaining control over the population in their communities. By the end of this period, leaders with genuine popular followings, like Zapata and Villa, had been assassinated, and control had been seized by a new postrevolutionary elite bent on demobilizing the masses and establishing the hegemony of the central government.

The rural aristocracy of the Porfiriato had been weakened but not eliminated; its heirs still controlled large concentrations of property and other forms of wealth in many parts of the country. Most of the large urban firms that operated during the Porfiriato also survived, further demonstrating that the revolution was not an attack on private capital per se.[6]

THE CÁRDENAS UPHEAVAL

Elite control was maintained during the 1930s, but this was nevertheless an era of massive social and political upheaval in Mexico. During the presidency of Lázaro Cárdenas (1934–1940), peasants

---

[5]Peter H. Smith, "The Making of the Mexican Constitution," in William O. Aydelotte, ed., *The History of Parliamentary Behavior* (Princeton, N.J.: Princeton University Press, 1977), p. 219.

[6]Stephen Haber, *Industry and Underdevelopment: The Industrialization of Mexico, 1890–1940* (Stanford, Calif.: Stanford University Press, 1988).

and urban workers succeeded for the first time in pressing their claims for land and higher wages; in fact, Cárdenas actively encouraged them to do so. The result was an unprecedented wave of strikes, protest demonstrations, and petitions for breaking up large rural estates.

Most disputes between labor and management during this period were settled, under government pressure, in favor of the workers. The Cárdenas administration also redistributed more than twice as much land as that expropriated by all of Cárdenas's predecessors since 1915, when Mexico's land reform program was formally initiated. By 1940 the country's land tenure system had been fundamentally altered, breaking the traditional domination of the large haciendas and creating a large sector of small peasant farmers called *ejidatarios*—more than 1.5 million of them—who had received plots of land under the agrarian reform program. The Cárdenas government actively encouraged the formation of new organizations of peasants and urban workers, grouped the new organizations into nationwide confederations, and provided arms to rural militias formed by the *ejidatarios* who had received plots of land redistributed by the government. Even Mexico's foreign relations were disrupted in 1938 when the Cárdenas government nationalized oil companies that had been operating in Mexico under U.S. and British ownership.

The Cárdenas era proved to be a genuine aberration in the development of postrevolutionary Mexico. Never before or since has the fundamental "who benefits?" question been addressed with such energy and commitment by a Mexican government. Mexican intellectuals frequently refer to 1938 as the high-water mark of the Mexican Revolution as measured by social progress, and characterize the period since then as a retrogression. Certainly, the distributive and especially the redistributive performance of the Mexican government declined sharply in the decades that followed, and the worker and peasant organizations formed during the Cárdenas era atrophied and became less and less likely to contest either the will of the government or the interests of Mexico's private economic elites. De facto reconcentration of land-holdings and other forms of wealth occurred as the state provided increasingly generous support to the country's new commercial, industrial, and financial elites during a period of rapid industrialization.

Critics of the Cárdenas administration have laid much of the blame for this outcome on the kind of mass political organizing that occurred under Cárdenas. The resulting organizations were captives of the regime—tied so closely to it that they had no capacity for autonomous action. Under the control of a new group of national political leaders whose values and priorities were unfavorable to the working classes, these same organizations, after Cárdenas, functioned only to enforce political stability and limit lower-class demands for government benefits. "The institutional shell of Cardenismo remained," writes historian Alan Knight, "but its internal dynamic was lost. In other words, the jalopy was hijacked by new drivers; they retuned the engine, took on new passengers, and then drove it in a quite different direction."[7]

Cárdenas represented a coalition of forces that was progressive but not committed to destroying the foundations of Mexican capitalism. While he was advised by left-wing Keynesian economists trained in England, Cárdenas himself was not a socialist. He may have considered socialism a desirable long-term goal, but neither he "nor his associates believed it was a realistic possibility for the immediate future."[8] His government's large investments in public works (electricity, roads, irrigation projects) and its reorganization of the country's financial system laid the foundations for the post-1940 "Mexican miracle" of rapid industrialization and low inflation within a capitalist framework. In the long term, the principal beneficiaries of Cárdenas's economic project proved to be the middle classes and unionized industrial workers—not peasants and the unorganized urban poor.

The Cárdenas era fundamentally reshaped Mexico's political institutions: The presidency became the primary institution of the political system, with sweeping powers exercised during a constitutionally limited six-year term with no possibility of reelection. The military was removed from overt political competition and transformed into one of several institutional pillars of the regime. And an elaborate network of government-sponsored peasant and labor organizations provided a mass base for the official political party and performed a variety of political and economic control functions, utilizing a multilayered system of patronage and clientelism.

By 1940 a much larger proportion of the Mexican population was nominally included in the national political system, mostly by their membership in peasant and labor organizations created by Cárdenas. No real democratization of the system resulted from this vast expansion of "political participation," however. Although working-class groups did have more control over their representatives in the government-sponsored organizations than over their former masters on the haciendas and in the factories, their influ-

---

[7] Alan Knight, "Cardenismo: Juggernaut or Jalopy?" *Journal of Latin American Studies* 26:1 (1994), p. 107.

[8] Nora Hamilton, *The Limits of State Autonomy: Post-Revolutionary Mexico* (Princeton, N.J.: Princeton University Press, 1982), p. 281.

ence over public policy and government priorities after Cárdenas was minimal and highly indirect. Policy recommendations, official actions, and nominations for elective and appointive positions at all levels still emanated from the central government and official party headquarters in Mexico City, filtering down the hierarchy to the rank and file for ratification and legitimation.

Cárdenas's experiment with democratization was centered in the workplace. Workers would participate in economic decision making in their *ejido* community or industrial plant. The outcome was greater workplace democracy during Cárdenas's presidency, but hardly the "workers' democracy" that in 1938 he claimed would be the end result of his political institution building.

The International Context

Since independence, Mexico's politics and public policies have always been influenced to some extent by proximity to the United States. Porfirio Díaz is widely reputed to have exclaimed, "Poor Mexico! So far from God and so close to the United States." Indeed, this proximity has made the United States a powerful presence in Mexico. The 2,000-mile land border between the two countries, Mexico's rich supplies of minerals, labor, and other resources needed by U.S. industry, and Mexico's attractiveness as a site for U.S. private investment made such influence inevitable.

Midway through the nineteenth century, Mexico's sovereignty as a nation was directly threatened when the United States' push for territorial and economic expansion met little resistance in northern Mexico. Emerging from a war for independence from Spain and plagued by chronic political instability, Mexico was highly vulnerable to aggression from the north. By annexing Texas in 1845 and instigating the Mexican American War of 1846–1848 (Ulysses S. Grant later called it "America's great unjust war"), the United States was able to seize half of Mexico's national territory: disputed land in Texas; all the land that is now California, Nevada, and Utah; most of New Mexico and Arizona; and part of Colorado and Wyoming. This massive seizure of territory, along with several later military interventions and meddling in the politics of "revolutionary" Mexico that extended through the 1920s, left scars that have not healed. Even today, the average Mexican suspects that the United States has designs on Mexico's remaining territory, its oil, even its human resources.

The lost territory includes the U.S. regions that have been the principal recipients of Mexican immigrant workers in this century. This labor migration, too, was instigated mainly by the United States. Beginning in the 1880s, U.S. farmers, railroads, and mining companies, with U.S. government encouragement, obtained many of the workers needed to expand the economy and transport systems of the Southwest and Midwest by sending labor recruiters into northern and central Mexico.

By the end of the 1920s, the economies of Mexico and the United States were sufficiently intertwined that the effects of the Great Depression were swiftly transmitted to Mexico, causing unemployment to rise and export earnings and gross national product (GNP) to plummet. In response to these economic shocks, Mexico tried during the 1930s to reduce its dependence on the United States as a market for silver and other exports. The effort failed, and by 1940 Mexico was more dependent than before on the flow of goods, capital, and labor to and from the United States.

After 1940, Mexico relied even more heavily on U.S. private capital to help finance its drive for industrialization. It was also during the 1940s, when the United States experienced severe shortages of labor in World War II, that Mexico's dependence on the United States as a market for its surplus labor became institutionalized through the so-called *bracero* program of importing contract labor. Operating from 1942 to 1964, this program brought more than 4 million Mexicans to the United States to work in seasonal agriculture. After the demise of the *bracero* program, migration to the United States continued, with most new arrivals entering illegally. The flow of migrant workers (and more recently, their dependents) has been so heavy in recent decades that by 1990 at least 5 percent of all people born in Mexico were living, more or less permanently, in the United States.[1]

The United States' stake in Mexico's continued political stability and economic development has increased dramatically since World War II. In recent years Mexico has been the third largest trading partner of the United States (behind Canada and Japan). Employment for hundreds of thousands of people in both Mexico and the United States depends on this trade. In 1982, when U.S. trade with Mexico fell by 32 percent because of Mexico's economic crisis, an estimated 250,000 jobs were lost in the United States. Largely because of the late 1994 peso devaluation, which made Mexico's exports cheaper in the United States and U.S. products unaffordable to most Mexican consumers, the overall U.S. trade deficit soared to record levels in the first quarter of 1995.

Despite the sharp fluctuations in Mexico's economy since the early 1980s, that country has become one of the preferred sites for investments by U.S.-based multinational corporations, especially for investments in modern industries like petrochemicals, pharmaceuticals, food processing, machinery, transportation, and ath-

[1] Rodolfo Corona, "Migración permanente interestatal e internacional, 1950–1990," *Comercio Exterior* 43:8 (1993), pp. 750–63.

letic footwear. Subsidiaries of U.S. companies produce half the manufactured goods exported by Mexico. Firms in Mexico's own private sector have actively sought foreign capital to finance new joint ventures and expand plant facilities. By the end of 1994, total U.S. investment in Mexico was more than $115 billion.

Mexico's external economic dependence has often been cited by both critics and defenders of the Mexican system as an all-encompassing explanation for the country's problems. In fact, economic ties between Mexico and the United States usually explain only part of the picture. And these linkages do not necessarily predetermine the choices of policy and development priorities that are set by Mexico's rulers. But Mexico's economic relationships with the United States clearly limit the range of choices that might be made by Mexican policy makers; and international economic fluctuations have become the largest source of uncertainty in Mexico's planning and policy making.

The crucial role played by foreign capital in Mexico's overall strategy of capitalist development makes it imperative for the Mexican state to maintain a favorable investment climate. Traditionally, it has done so by imposing discipline and wage restraint on Mexico's labor force (through government-controlled labor unions), providing generous fiscal incentives and infrastructure for investors (both foreign and domestic), keeping taxes low, and maintaining political stability. More recently, foreign capital has been courted by liberalizing regulations for such investment (allowing up to 100 percent foreign ownership of many new firms, versus the traditional limit of 49 percent) and opening up most sectors of the economy to foreign investment—including sectors formerly reserved for domestic investors or the government itself.

Beginning in 1990, the Mexican government added to these incentives by proposing a U.S.–Mexico–Canada free trade agreement, which would make Mexico a more attractive investment site for U.S. firms seeking low-cost labor and for Asian and European firms seeking privileged access to the U.S. market. While Carlos Salinas opposed such an agreement during his 1988 presidential campaign, because "there is such a different economic level between the U.S. and Mexico," he soon found himself with no alternative to pursuing greater economic integration with the United States. With 1 million new job seekers entering its labor force each year, Mexico desperately needed to increase its rate of economic growth, and the only way to do that while containing inflation was to stimulate a massive new infusion of investment capital from abroad. After an intense debate in the United States, the North American Free Trade Agreement (NAFTA) was approved by the U.S. Congress in November 1993.

Little more than a year later, the implications of much closer linkage between the U.S. and Mexican economies became painfully clear, when a new financial crisis erupted in Mexico. While there was virtually no political constituency within the United States for a U.S. government "bailout" of Mexico, and no enthusiasm among Mexicans for taking on more foreign loans and using the country's oil revenues to collateralize them (just one of the stringent conditions imposed by the United States), neither government had any realistic alternative to such a rescue. A Mexican default on repayment of nearly $30 billion in *tesobonos* (short-term bonds issued by the Mexican treasury) held mostly by U.S. pension funds, mutual funds, and other institutional investors would have threatened the assets of many millions of American households whose money had been invested in the high-yielding Mexican government bonds. Moreover, a meltdown of the Mexican economy could have caused a dramatic surge in the number of Mexicans immigrating illegally to the United States, in addition to those who will be coming because of the 1994–95 peso devaluation, which made the U.S. minimum wage more than 12 times higher than Mexico's. Consequently, a nearly $50 billion multilateral package of loan guarantees and credit line swaps—including $20 billion from a U.S. government currency stabilization fund—was made available to Mexico in January 1995.

As the U.S. and Mexican economies have become more closely intertwined, scrutiny of Mexico's political process by U.S. officials and the U.S. media has increased. The flawed macroeconomic policies that contributed crucially to Mexico's economic crises of the 1980s and 1990s eroded U.S. confidence in the Mexican government and raised concern about its ability to maintain political stability. Simultaneously, the United States' heightened preoccupation with illicit drugs—most of which now reach the United States via Mexico—has led members of the U.S. Congress and other officials to harshly criticize police and government corruption in Mexico, which is a significant facilitator of the drug traffic. Finally, as Mexican opposition parties and nongovernmental organizations increasingly turned to the U.S. mass media and the U.S. Congress to voice complaints about electoral fraud by the PRI-government apparatus, the halting and incomplete character of Mexico's democratization became an issue in U.S.-Mexican relations. In 1994, in an effort to rebuild the credibility of its electoral system, the Mexican government agreed for the first time to permit foreign observers to scrutinize the August 21 national elections.

Political Structure and Institutions

Mexico's political system has long defied easy classification. In the 1950s and 1960s some U.S. political scientists depicted the regime as a one-party democracy that was evolving toward "true" (North Atlantic–style) democracy. Certain imperfections were recognized, but in the view of these analysts, political development in Mexico was simply incomplete. After the government's massacre of student protesters in 1968, most analysts began describing the system as authoritarian, but even this characterization was subject to qualification. Mexico now seems to belong to that rapidly expanding category of hybrid, part-free, part-authoritarian systems that do not conform to classical typologies.[1] Such labels as selective democracy, hard-line democracy, *democradura* (a Spanish contraction of "democracy" and "dictatorship"), and modernizing authoritarian regime have been applied to such systems.[2] They are characterized by competitive (though not necessarily fair and honest) elections that install governments more committed to maintaining political stability and labor discipline than to expanding democratic freedoms, protecting human rights, or mediating class conflicts. Some regimes of this type are more likely to countenance undemocratic practices and procedures (for example, electoral fraud, selective repression of dissidents) than others.

For most of the period since 1940, Mexico has had a pragmatic and moderate authoritarian regime, not the zealously repressive kind that emerged in Latin America's southern cone in the 1960s

---

[1] See Lucian W. Pye, "Political Science and the Crisis of Authoritarianism," *American Political Science Review* 84:1 (March 1990), pp. 3–19.

[2] Guillermo O'Donnell, Philippe C. Schmitter, and Laurence Whitehead, eds., *Transitions from Authoritarian Rule* (Baltimore, Md.: Johns Hopkins University Press, 1986); Catherine M. Conaghan and Rosario Espinal, "Unlikely Transitions to Uncertain Regimes? — Democracy Without Compromise in the Dominican Republic and Ecuador," *Journal of Latin American Studies* 22:3 (October 1990), pp. 553–74; and Peter H. Smith, "Crisis and Democracy in Latin America," *World Politics* 43:4 (July 1991), pp. 608–34.

and 1970s. It has been an institutional system, not a personalistic instrument, which has dealt successfully with one of the most difficult problems for nondemocratic systems: elite renewal and executive succession. The Mexican system has been inclusionary, given to co-optation and incorporation rather than exclusion or elimination of troublesome political forces. (President Salinas's attempt to completely marginalize the Cardenista left during his term is a conspicuous exception to this historical pattern.) It strives to incorporate the broadest possible range of social, economic, and political interests within the official party, its affiliated "mass" organizations, and opposition groups whose activities are sanctioned by the regime. As potentially dissident groups have appeared, their leaders usually have been co-opted into government-controlled organizations, or new organizations have been established under government auspices as vehicles for emerging interests. However, when confronted with unco-optable opposition groups or movements (for example, students in 1968; the Cardenista left from 1987 to 1994; the Zapatista rebels in Chiapas since January 1, 1994), the regime has responded punitively.

On paper, the Mexican government appears to be structured much like the U.S. government: a presidential system, three autonomous branches of government (executive, legislative, judicial) with checks and balances, and federalism with considerable autonomy at the local (municipal) level. In practice, however, Mexico's system of government was far removed from the U.S. model. Decision making has been highly centralized. The president, operating with relatively few restraints on his authority, completely dominated the legislative and judicial branches. Both houses of the federal legislature have been controlled continuously by members affiliated with the ruling PRI. Opposition party members could criticize the government and its policies vociferously, but their objections to proposals initiated by the president and backed by his party rarely affected the final shape of legislation. Courts and legislatures at the state level normally mirrored the preferences of the state governors, who themselves were handpicked by the incumbent president.

At all levels of the system, the overwhelming majority of those elected to public office have been, in effect, political appointees—named to their positions by higher-ups within the PRI-government apparatus. Until recently, selection as the candidate of the official party was tantamount to election, except in a handful of municipalities and congressional districts where opposition parties were so strong that they could not be ignored. Those elected on the PRI ticket have been accountable and responsive not primarily to the people who elected them but to their political patrons within the regime. Most citizens who bothered to vote did so with little or no expectation that their votes would influence the outcome of the election, nor the subsequent behavior of the winner. The winner, they realized, had been predetermined by the selection process within the PRI, which until recently has had little grassroots input. Instead, nominating conventions—if held at all—were attended only by party activists, whose role was to ratify the choices made in private by officials at higher levels.

These and other features of the Mexican system as it operated at least through 1994 are common to authoritarian regimes elsewhere: limited (not responsible) pluralism; low popular mobilization, with most citizen participation in the electoral process mobilized by the government itself; competition for public office and government benefits restricted mainly to those who support the system; centralized, often arbitrary decision making by one leader or small group; weak ideological constraints on public policy making; extensive government manipulation of the mass media. As mentioned above, however, the Mexican system is more complex than most of the authoritarian regimes that have ruled other Third World nations in recent decades, and its internal arrangements are in flux.

In 1988 the ruling party's control of the Congress was weakened significantly, setting the stage for a new era in executive-legislative relations. Sixty-six PRI candidates for seats in the lower house of Congress were defeated in that year's national elections—nearly as many as the total of ruling party candidates defeated in all elections between 1946 and 1985. For the 1988–1991 period, the PRI was reduced to a bare working majority in the Chamber of Deputies (260 out of 500 seats), and for the first time since the ruling party was founded in 1929, opposition party candidates were elected to the Senate (4 out of 64 seats). Because the PRI no longer commanded a two-thirds majority in the lower house, President Salinas temporarily had to negotiate with the opposition party delegations (he chose to deal only with the PAN) to secure passage of key legislation amending the constitution.[3]

Moreover, the Congress had ceased to function as a reliable instrument for the internal distribution of power and its perks within the ruling party. With the recognition of so many opposition victories for congressional seats in 1988, aspiring PRIistas had to face the reality that nomination by their party was no longer equivalent to election. The tradition of the *carro completo* (clean sweep) by PRI candidates was clearly threatened.

---

[3] In the 1991 congressional elections, the PRI, buoyed by the popularity of President Salinas and his National Solidarity Program of public works and social welfare spending, increased its majority in the Chamber of Deputies to 320 seats.

TABLE 1
COMPOSITION OF THE MEXICAN CONGRESS, 1994–1997

	Won by Majority Vote	Awarded by P.R. System	Total	%
Chamber of Deputies				
PRI	274	27[a]	301	60.8
PAN	19	99	118	23.9
PRD	5	64	69	12.9
PT	0	10	10	2.0
Annulled elections[b]	2	—	2	0.4
Total	300	200	500	100.0
Senate[c]				
PRI	95	0	95	74.2
PAN	1	24	25	19.5
PRD	0	8	8	6.3
Total	96	32	128	100.0

PRI — Partido Revolucionario Institucional   PAN — Partido Acción Nacional
PRD — Partido de la Revolución Democrática   PT — Partido del Trabajo

[a]Includes two seats provisionally assigned to the Partido Revolucionario Institucional, pending the results of special elections to be held in districts where results of the August 1994 elections were annulled.

[b]Seats corresponding to congressional districts in which the results of the August 1994 elections were annulled.

[c]Includes 32 senators serving terms running from 1991 to 1997, as well as those elected to serve from 1994 to 2000.

Source: Instituto Federal Electoral, *1994: Tu elección—memoria del proceso electoral federal* (México, D.F.: Instituto Federal Electoral, 1995), tables 8.1 and 8.2, pp. 367–68.

The Congress was further transformed by electoral law reforms enacted in 1993, which had the effect of greatly increasing the representation of opposition parties in the Senate. The Senate was doubled in size (to 128 members), and the reforms guaranteed that the opposition parties, combined, would control at least one-quarter of the seats, as compared with less than 5 percent during the 1988–1993 period. The 1994 elections also expanded somewhat the opposition parties' presence in the Chamber of Deputies, to 200 out of 500 seats, though only 24 of the opposition-held seats were won by majority vote in the congressional districts; the remainder were awarded to the opposition parties through a proportional representation formula (see table 1).

Considerably more important than the size of the opposition party delegations in the Congress today is the way in which President Zedillo has chosen to handle his relations with the legislative branch, which has brought some stunning changes. As part of an overall strategy to broaden the base of support for his administration, Zedillo has offered to share power with the Congress in several key areas. Shortly after taking office, Zedillo invited all 500 newly elected members of the Chamber of Deputies to a luncheon, thus becoming the first president in 65 years of PRI rule to have a direct dialogue with the members of Congress, including those representing opposition parties. At that historic meeting, Zedillo announced his "commitment to forge a new balance of powers," and he challenged the deputies to assert their constitutionally prescribed authority as never before. He subsequently proposed congressional approval of all major judicial appointments, as well as oversight of all federal government spending by a new auditing agency under congressional control.

The Congress, including the PRI's delegation, has responded to Zedillo's challenge. In March 1995, after some 50 PRI deputies threatened to vote against a key element of the government's postdevaluation austerity plan—a 50 percent increase in the value-added tax, which is levied on virtually all goods and services—Zedillo found it necessary to aggressively lobby the congressional leaders of his own party to secure approval of the much despised measure. Only Zedillo's arm-twisting, combined with PRIistas' fears that the president would begin working directly with opposition party members if his own party split on this crucial vote, prevented a wholesale breakdown of party discipline.

If Zedillo's commitment to a more equal balance of executive and legislative powers is sustained, he and future presidents will have to lobby and negotiate with the Congress—including members of the PRI—on a routine basis. Coalition building with opposition party members will become more frequent. The era when Congress's sole functions were to serve as a debating arena for the opposition parties and as a rubber stamp for decisions already taken by the president may have ended.

POLITICAL CENTRALISM

Despite the federalist structure of government that is enshrined in the 1917 constitution and legal codes, with their emphasis on the *municipio libre* (the concept of the free municipality, able to control its own affairs), in practice the Mexican political system has usually functioned in a highly centralized manner. From the 1920s through the Salinas presidency, the concentration of decision-making power at the federal level in most policy areas was continuous. Control over elections—placed entirely at the municipal and state levels by the initial postrevolutionary electoral code, enacted in 1918—also passed to agencies that were part of the federal government apparatus or state-level entities controlled by federal authorities.[4] A high degree of political centralism has been considered one of the main factors underlying Mexico's long-term political stability, although recent research at the regional level has demonstrated that political control by the center has been far less complete than is commonly assumed.[5]

Mexico is divided into 32 states and federal territories, and each state is divided into *municipios* (politico-administrative units roughly equivalent in size and governmental functions to county governments in the United States). The *municipio* is governed by an *ayuntamiento*, or council, headed by a *presidente municipal* (municipal president or mayor). Municipal officials are elected every three years. Traditionally, each *presidente municipal* has been handpicked by higher-ups within the PRI-government apparatus, normally a federal congressman and the state governor.

The absence of popular input into this candidate selection process has often led to the designation of municipal presidents who were intensely disliked by their constituents, and who embarrassed the PRI and the government by their inept handling of local problems. Such outcomes have led to several short-lived experiments with open primary elections, to compel would-be PRI candidates for municipal president or state governor to develop a popular support base. Each of these experiments, occurring under Presidents Gustavo Díaz Ordaz (in the mid-1960s), Miguel de la Madrid (mid-1980s), and Carlos Salinas (early 1990s), was abandoned after fierce resistance by old-guard PRI leaders and, in Salinas's case, when candidates preferred by the president were defeated in primary elections by local favorites.

Since the opposition parties (most notably, the PAN) began to nominate their candidates at highly publicized, open conventions, the PRI is under increasing pressure to follow their example. Having been told repeatedly by President Zedillo that he will not interfere in the party's candidate selection processes, PRI leaders in several states encouraged multiple, competing candidacies for governorships to be filled in 1995 and held conventions attended by thousands of delegates to select the party's nominees. It remains to be seen whether Zedillo's break with the tradition of imposing candidates from above will, in fact, make

---

[4]With passage of the Electoral Law of 1946, the preparation, conduct, and validation of elections at all levels were placed under federal control.

[5]See Richard R. Fagen and William S. Tuohy, *Politics and Privilege in a Mexican City* (Stanford, Calif.: Stanford University Press, 1972), pp. 18–41; Alan Knight, "Historical Continuities in Social Movements," in Joe Foweraker and Ann L. Craig, eds., *Popular Movements and Political Change in Mexico* (Boulder, Colo.: Lynne Rienner, 1990), pp. 78–102; and Jeffrey W. Rubin, "Decentering the Regime: Culture and Regional Politics in Mexico," *Latin American Research Review*, forthcoming.

elective positions accessible to all PRI militants. Even if liberated from "guidance" from Mexico City, many of the entrenched state- and local-level party bosses will try to manipulate the PRI's nomination processes in order to protect their authoritarian enclaves. This is exactly what happened in the state of Yucatán in 1995, where one of the PRI's most notorious "dinosaurs" succeeded in having the state's constitution changed to make him eligible to run for governor, an office that he had previously held on an interim (presidentially appointed) basis. Some analysts have used the term "Yugoslavization" to describe the tensions emerging between this and other old-style, state-level PRI machines and the central government.

The ongoing rebellion in Chiapas is a forceful reminder of the potential for local and regional conflicts to spill over into the national political arena. Regional particularism has been a constant in Mexican politics since the mid-nineteenth century, but it has been especially potent during periods in which the central government is perceived as being less efficacious and legitimate.[6] The economic crisis of the 1980s brought a resurgence of political regionalism, fueled by growing public resentment of heavy-handed rule from Mexico City, which has not abated.

The grievances of the provinces have been exploited successfully by opposition parties, especially the PAN. Regional pride, combined with the increasing rejection by business elites of control by a failing central government, became a major source of PAN strength in municipal and gubernatorial elections held during the 1980s in the northern border states. In 1983, for example, the PAN swept to victory in all major cities of Chihuahua, containing more than 70 percent of the state's population. In the state of Baja California in 1989, the vote for the PAN's gubernatorial candidate, Ernesto Ruffo, was so overwhelming that the federal government was virtually compelled to recognize his victory. The Mexico City–based political elite, which in recent decades has been dominated increasingly by people born or raised in the capital,[7] has not been oblivious to these trends. The Salinas government took a generally cooperative, nonconfrontational stance toward the PANista government of Baja California State, hoping to demonstrate that Mexico City could

---

[6]See Edward J. Williams, "The Resurgent North and Contemporary Mexican Regionalism," *Mexican Studies* 6:2 (Summer 1990), pp. 299–323; and Eric Van Young, ed., *Mexico's Regions: Comparative History and Development* (La Jolla: Center for U.S.-Mexican Studies, University of California, San Diego, 1992).

[7]See Peter H. Smith, *Labyrinths of Power: Political Recruitment in Twentieth Century Mexico* (Princeton, N.J.: Princeton University Press, 1979), p. 306; and Miguel Angel Centeno, *Democracy within Reason: Technocratic Revolution in Mexico* (University Park: Pennsylvania State University Press, 1994), p. 112.

work constructively with at least some kinds of opposition governments in the periphery.

Nevertheless, the legacy of political centralism is still dramatically evident in Mexico today. Each successive layer of government is significantly weaker, less autonomous, and more impoverished than the levels above it. Historically, the federal government has controlled about 85 percent of public revenues, the state governments have controlled less than 12 percent, and the *municipios* scarcely 3 percent. By 1994, the *municipios'* share of total public spending had risen to 4 percent, and the states' share to 16 percent. The federal government still took in 98 percent of all public revenues obtained through taxation, while the states collected 1.5 percent and the *municipios*, 0.5 percent.[8] Municipal governments controlled by the PAN have had much greater success in increasing self-generated revenues than those controlled by the PRI, which typically defer to the federal government.[9] They may also resist collecting higher taxes for the federal government. In 1995, for example, the state legislatures of Jalisco and Yucatán, now controlled by the PAN, called upon the federal Congress to reverse the Zedillo government's 50 percent increase in the value-added tax.

All of Mexico's six most recent presidents entered office pledging to renew the "struggle against centralism," but serious efforts to decentralize have been made only since 1984. Under de la Madrid and Salinas, a limited form of revenue sharing was implemented and the federal constitution was amended to enhance the capacity of local governments to raise their own revenues. Partially successful efforts were also made to shift decision-making authority over public education and health care from the federal government to the states.[10] On the other hand, the Salinas administration's National Solidarity Program (PRONASOL)—its principal social program, reaching into more than

---

[8]Tonatiuh Guillén López, "La transición democrática en Baja California: los límites de la reproducción de un partido de oposición en el poder," paper presented at the Center for U.S.-Mexican Studies, University of California, San Diego, January 20, 1995.

[9]See Victoria E. Rodríguez and Peter M. Ward, *Policymaking, Politics, and Urban Governance in Chihuahua: The Experience of Recent PANista Governments* (Austin: LBJ School of Public Affairs, University of Texas at Austin, 1992); Rodríguez and Ward, *Political Change in Baja California: Democracy in the Making?* (La Jolla: Center for U.S.-Mexican Studies, University of California, San Diego, 1995); and Rodríguez and Ward, eds., *Opposition Government in Mexico* (Albuquerque: University of New Mexico Press, 1995).

[10]See John J. Bailey, *Governing Mexico: The Statecraft of Crisis Management* (New York: St. Martin's Press, 1988), pp. 83–86; and Victoria Rodríguez, "The Politics of Decentralization in Mexico: From Municipio Libre to Solidaridad," *Bulletin of Latin American Research* 12:2 (1993).

95 percent of the country's 2,378 municipalities—was structured and administered in such a way that it reinforced highly centralized presidential rule.[11]

More assertively than any of his predecessors, President Zedillo has vowed to reduce centralism, going so far as to sign an agreement with the country's state governors and mayors calling for constitutional amendments that would provide the legal framework for "a new Mexican federalism." Zedillo has promised a more equitable distribution of federal funds to the states, and a devolution of some functions that have been usurped by the federal government. Almost immediately, the president's commitment to a "new federalism" was put to the test by a group of border-city mayors, affiliated with both the PAN and the PRI, who began taking over the highly lucrative tollbooths on bridges in their cities that are used by vehicles crossing into the United States, and refusing to remit any of the revenues collected to the federal treasury. The mayor of Ciudad Juárez, adjacent to El Paso, Texas, was promptly jailed by federal officials for this offense, even as Zedillo's Interior Ministry was sponsoring public forums in every state capital to discuss ideas for implementing "the new federalism." Some federal ministries, especially the Treasury Ministry, continue to resist further revenue sharing with municipal governments, on the grounds that they lack the administrative capacity to make effective use of additional resources.

The state governors represent another potential obstacle to Zedillo's "new federalism." The governors retain control over all resources transferred from the federal government, and effective administrative decentralization down to the *municipio* level would require them to relinquish a major portion of their political power—something that they have successfully resisted. It is clear that, even under a president strongly committed to redistributing resources and sharing power with subnational units of government, movement toward U.S.-style federalism in Mexico will meet with opposition from many different quarters, including the federal government and the states themselves.

THE PRESIDENCY

Mexico's political system is commonly described as presidentialist or presidentially centered. The Mexican president possesses a broad range of both constitutionally mandated and unwritten but

---

[11]See John Bailey, "Centralism and Political Change in Mexico: The Case of National Solidarity," in Wayne A. Cornelius, Ann L. Craig, and Jonathan Fox, eds., *Transforming State-Society Relations in Mexico: The National Solidarity Strategy* (La Jolla: Center for U.S.-Mexican Studies, University of California, San Diego, 1994), pp. 97–119.

generally recognized "metaconstitutional" powers that traditionally have assured his dominance over all of the country's other
political institutions.[12] For example, on any issue of national
political significance, the federal judiciary could be expected to
take its cue from the incumbent president. Presidential decrees or
legislation enacted at the behest of the president were never found
to be unconstitutional by the Supreme Court, and presidential
appointments to or dismissals from the federal judiciary were
never challenged by the Congress. Thus, upon taking office,
President Zedillo was able to replace the entire Supreme Court that
he inherited from the Salinas administration, as part of an ambitious project to reduce corruption throughout the judicial system.

Since 1929 the president has also functioned as the "supreme
head" of the official party, choosing its leaders, dictating his
legislative proposals to the PRI delegation in Congress (and expect-
ing them to be approved with near unanimity), shaping the party's
internal governance, imposing his personal choices for the PRI's
gubernatorial and congressional candidates, and—most importantly—controlling the selection of the party's next presidential
nominee.

Since the 1920s, a great part of the Mexican president's power
has derived from his ability to seat and unseat state governors,
mayors (including the mayor of Mexico City, who is an unelected,
presidential appointee), and members of Congress. Indeed, all but
a handful of public officeholders in Mexico—primarily elected
officials affiliated with opposition parties—serve at the pleasure of
the president. Under Salinas, 17 state governors resigned, most
under pressure from Los Pinos (the Mexican "White House"). The
president can even remove the leaders of large, government-
affiliated labor unions, as Carlos Salinas demonstrated within
several months of taking office by sacking two of Mexico's most
powerful, corrupt, and independent-minded labor chieftains, who
had long headed the petroleum workers' and teachers' unions.
Mexicans use the term *presidencialismo* to connote this extraordinary concentration of powers, formal and informal, in the hands of
the Mexican president—and the implication that incumbents fre-

---

[12]For a conventional interpretation of the powers of the Mexican president, see Luis
Javier Garrido, "The Crisis of *Presidencialismo*," in Wayne A. Cornelius, Judith
Gentleman, and Peter H. Smith, eds., *Mexico's Alternative Political Futures* (La Jolla:
Center for U.S.-Mexican Studies, University of California, San Diego, 1989), pp.
417–34. A more nuanced view, emphasizing the various institutional mechanisms
that have made strong presidential rule possible in Mexico, is provided in Jeffrey
Weldon, "The Logic of *Presidencialismo* in Mexico," in Scott Mainwaring and
Matthew S. Shugart, eds., *Presidentialism and Democracy in Latin America* (Cam-
bridge and New York: Cambridge University Press, forthcoming).

quently abuse these powers in pursuit of personal and political ends.

The absence of a rigid, fully elaborated political ideology has made it possible for a Mexican president to have a pragmatic, flexible program and style of governance. The so-called ideology of the Mexican Revolution is little more than a loosely connected set of goals or symbols: social justice, economic nationalism, restrictions on the influence of the church in public life, and freedom from self-perpetuating, dictatorial rule in the Porfirio Díaz style. There are a few tenets of "revolutionary" ideology that must still be scrupulously observed, such as the constitutionally mandated no-reelection principle: No official, at any level of the system, can be reelected to the same public office, at least for consecutive terms; the president himself is limited to a single, six-year term.[13] Virtually all other elements of revolutionary ideology have been compromised or ignored, at one time or another, by the presidents holding office since 1940. Under Presidents de la Madrid and Salinas, for example, the definition of economic nationalism shifted drastically from keeping U.S. interests at bay to achieving competitiveness and new markets for Mexico's exports in the world economy, through policies aimed at opening up the Mexican economy to more foreign-made products and foreign direct investment, and linking Mexico's economy even more closely to that of the United States.

Even though the Mexican president unquestionably wields great power, his autonomy can be limited in certain policy domains. For example, President Luis Echeverría often blamed his economic policy failures on the machinations of the business elite centered in the city of Monterrey, and there is credible evidence that, in 1972, big business forced Echeverría to drop his plan to increase the tax burden on the wealthy.[14] Similarly, the private sector appears to have vetoed a relatively modest income tax increase that was to have been included in President Zedillo's March 1995 austerity plan. Zedillo deleted the income tax hike from the package, substituting for it a much steeper, more regressive increase in the value-added (sales) tax.

---

[13] At various times during his *sexenio*, it was widely rumored that President Salinas wished to abolish the constitutional prohibition on reelection of the president, thereby enabling himself to serve two terms. Even if this was Salinas's preference, the political furor unleashed by the floating of this trial balloon by some of his aides apparently caused him to abandon the idea.

[14] See Leopoldo Solís, *Economic Policy Reform in Mexico* (New York: Pergamon, 1981), pp. 73–76. On the Monterrey business elite and its own contentious relationship with the central government, see Alex M. Saragoza, *The Monterrey Elite and the Mexican State, 1880–1940* (Austin: University of Texas Press, 1988).

By the late 1980s, conventional wisdom held that traditional Mexican *presidencialismo*—especially if defined as the ability of the president to take unilateral actions that may be damaging to the interests of political and economic elites—was dead, the victim of the excesses and leadership failures of the last three presidents. Upon taking office in December 1988, Carlos Salinas challenged this notion through a succession of bold strokes against the fiefdoms that had increasingly challenged presidential prerogatives during the preceding four administrations (for instance, the oil workers' union), and by embracing new policies that entailed large political risks (including a free trade agreement with the United States and Canada). These actions proved that the essential powers of Mexican *presidencialismo* were still intact and could be used to effect sweeping political and economic change. Salinas's successful effort to privatize all but a handful of state-owned enterprises also liberated resources (previously used to subsidize inefficient, money-losing public-sector firms) that could be used to fund large new "presidentialist" programs, like National Solidarity, which were administered directly through the office of the president.

Salinas's successor, Ernesto Zedillo, seems to be laying the groundwork for a very different kind of *presidencialismo*—one that will have to rely more on skillful negotiation and alliance building with actors throughout the political system. Zedillo has steadfastly refused to assume the president's traditional role as leader of the PRI. He has publicly pledged, on numerous occasions, to refrain from interfering in internal party matters, including candidate selection. He has committed himself to working with the opposition party delegations in the Congress, not just with the PRI majority. He also served notice that, unlike his predecessors, he would not involve himself in adjudicating disputed elections, thereby serving notice to the PRI that the president could no longer be relied upon to be the ultimate guarantor of the party's electoral victories. Finally, Zedillo approved the arrest and jailing of Raúl Salinas, a brother of the ex-president, on charges of having masterminded the assassination of the PRI's second-ranking official in September 1994 (possibly an effort to conceal illicit, private business dealings that were known to the victim). In doing so, Zedillo broke the "rule of impunity" that has always protected former presidents, their close relatives, and principal aides from prosecution for corruption or politically motivated crimes committed during their terms. This stunning violation of precedent made Zedillo himself, and his successors, vulnerable to similar treatment once they leave office.

President Carlos Salinas de Gortari (1988–1994) greeting beneficiaries of his administration's National Solidarity Program. Source: *Office of the President, Mexico.*

Indeed, so many presidential prerogatives were abdicated by Zedillo, during his electoral campaign and in the first months of his presidency, that concerns were soon being expressed about his ability to govern the country and prevent the PRI from tearing itself apart. Zedillo's hands-off stance toward the PRI also has serious implications for his ability to move the country toward full democracy. Left to its own devices, the PRI may be more likely to nominate old-guard, antireform "dinosaurs" as candidates for state governorships and congressional seats. Party discipline may break down in the Congress, complicating the approval of constitutional amendments (which require a two-thirds majority vote) and other key legislation needed to advance the president's programs, including further reforms of the electoral system. PRI state governors, whatever their transgressions and however fraud-tainted their electoral victories may have been, will be emboldened to resist presidential efforts to remove them. After all, if PRIista officeholders no longer owe their positions to the president, and cannot depend on him to guarantee their election (regardless of the actual results), why should they follow his lead?

If the president no longer exercises effective control over his own party, he may not have the capacity to make good on commitments made to opposition parties. For example, Zedillo reportedly gave private assurances to leaders of the center-left Partido de la Revolución Democrática (PRD) that conflicts spawned by the 1994 gubernatorial elections in the states of Chiapas and Tabasco—the results of which were strongly challenged by the PRD—would be settled in ways acceptable to the Perredistas. He delivered on that promise in Chiapas, forcing the elected PRI governor to take an indefinite "leave of absence." But in Tabasco, Zedillo's attempt to remove a PRI governor whose election was badly tainted by vote fraud and wildly excessive campaign spending was blocked by an open rebellion of local PRI militants, supported by the party's national leaders. In short, Zedillo's effort to distance himself and his government from the PRI, coupled with his commitment to a "new federalism," could become a major stumbling block to further democratization.[15]

There will be many tests of Zedillo's resolve to recast the institution of the presidency, but the most important will come as his term is ending. Tradition dictates that, at that point, he would exercise his metaconstitutional power as incumbent president to select his own successor, with minimal input from other key actors in the ruling coalition. In September 1990 Luis Echeverría became the first former president to publicly acknowledge this crucially important, unwritten rule of the Mexican political system.[16]

Also by tradition, those who aspire to the PRI's presidential nomination cannot openly campaign for it, or even admit that they are seeking the presidency. The supporters of the major contenders work diligently behind the scenes to advance their man's prospects and to discredit other contenders. In 1987, in response to widespread criticism of the traditional, secretive selection process, Miguel de la Madrid, acting through the nominal head of the PRI, publicly identified six "distinguished party members" as precandidates for the PRI's 1988 presidential nomination, and he arranged for them to present their ideas to PRI notables at semipublic breakfast meetings. These appearances represented only a cosmetic change in the presidential succession process, however, since they provoked no real debate or public campaigning by the hopefuls, and the outgoing president remained firmly in control of the nomination process.

---

[15]See Alonso Lujambio, "Federalismo y sistema de partidos en la transición," *Este País* 34 (January 1994), pp. 20–22.

[16]For attempts to codify the informal rules of presidential succession in Mexico, see Smith, *Labyrinths of Power*, chap. 10; Peter H. Smith, "The 1988 Presidential Succession in Historical Perspective," in Cornelius, Gentleman, and Smith, eds., *Mexico's Alternative Political Futures*, chap. 17; and Luis Javier Garrido, "Las quince reglas de la sucesión presidencial," in Abraham Nuncio, ed., *La sucesión presidencial en 1988* (México, D.F.: Grijalbo, 1988).

In choosing two of his cabinet members, initially Luis Donaldo Colosio and, following his assassination, Ernesto Zedillo to succeed him, Carlos Salinas dispensed with such cosmetic measures. The process through which the PRI's presidential candidates were selected in 1993 and 1994 was as closed and secretive as ever, even though Salinas's imposition of Zedillo to replace the slain Colosio was briefly and openly resisted by the PRI hierarchy. But public scrutiny of Salinas's second-choice candidate was expanded enormously by Zedillo's participation in the first-ever, face-to-face, nationally televised debate among the principal presidential candidates. According to post-debate opinion surveys, Zedillo was soundly defeated by the PAN's highly articulate candidate, Diego Fernández de Cevallos. Fernández failed to capitalize on his victory, partly because of a government-orchestrated media blackout of his activities during the week following the debate, and Zedillo went on to win a decisive victory at the polls on August 21. But the mere fact that a PRI presidential candidate had agreed to debate directly with his opponents on national television was a major, probably irreversible step toward a more democratic presidential succession.

CAMARILLAS AND CLIENTELISM

The Mexican political class is permeated with patron-client relationships, in which the "patrons"—persons having higher political status—provide benefits such as protection, support in political struggles with rivals, and chances for upward political or economic mobility to their "clients"—persons with a lower political status. In exchange, the "clients" provide loyalty, deference, and useful services like voter mobilization, political control, and problem solving to their patrons within the official party or governmental bureaucracy.[17]

The chains of patron-client relationships are interwoven because patrons do not want to limit themselves to one client, and clients avoid pinning all their hopes on a single patron. Normally, these interlocking chains of clientage relationships come together at the apex of the national authority structure—the presidency. For all those who hold office during a given *sexenio* (six-year presidential term), the president is the supreme patron. When this is not the case, as during the struggle between followers of *líder máximo* Plutarco Elías Calles and President Lázaro Cárdenas in 1935–1936

---

[17]Clientelistic relationships are by no means limited to the political elite. For an analysis of the importance of clientelism as a way of structuring interaction and control throughout Mexican society, see Luis Roniger, *Hierarchy and Trust in Modern Mexico and Brazil* (New York: Praeger, 1990).

Participants in the first-ever, nationally televised debate among Mexican presidential candidates, held in July 1994 (left to right: Ernesto Zedillo, PRI candidate; Diego Fernández de Cevallos, PAN candidate; Cuauhtémoc Cárdenas, PRD candidate; front-center, television moderator. Source: Cuartoscuro Photo-Pedro Valtierra; by permission of Secretaría de Gobernación, Mexico.

and the conflict between Salinistas and Zedillistas in 1995–1996, there is potential for political instability. Discipline within the ruling elite breaks down, and all officeholders must choose sides.

The vertical grouping of several different levels of patron-client relationships is popularly known in Mexico as a *camarilla*—roughly translated, a "political clique" (see figure 1). The largest and most important *camarillas*—those reaching into the presidential cabinet—typically have been assembled over a long period of time, through an elaborate process of personal alliance building. At the cabinet level, the *camarillas* vie constantly for influence over national policy making in key areas. Above all, throughout the *sexenio* they jockey for position in the race for the presidency itself. The cabinet ministers who lead the rival *camarillas* are often, themselves, aspirants to the presidency.

Because reelection to the presidency is prohibited, the supreme patron in this elaborate clientage structure is replaced every six years. The new president has his own *camarilla*, whose members, in turn, have different followers of their own, and so on down the system. The government-wide shuffling of officeholders at the beginning of each new presidential administration actually amounts to substituting one major *camarilla*—the one that will now control the presidency—for another (the one headed by the outgo-

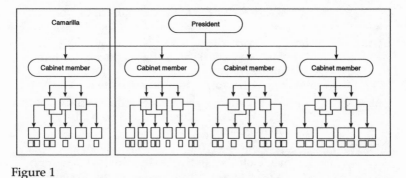

Figure 1

CLIENTAGE STRUCTURES WITHIN THE MEXICAN POLITICAL ELITE

ing president). The basic element that binds *camarillas* together is personal loyalty to the *camarilla* leader rather than ideology. The members of the winning *camarilla* may, indeed, share certain policy preferences or career experiences that distinguish them from previous administrations, but the essential bond is loyalty to the man who holds the presidency, from whom all policy and stylistic cues are taken.

One major consequence of this kind of political elite structure is that the responsiveness and accountability of officials to the ruling party's ostensible "mass constituencies" (organized in labor unions, peasant confederations, urban popular movements, and the like) and to the general public is greatly diminished. Fervent, unquestioning loyalty and service to one's immediate superior in the PRI-government apparatus is the only promising route to upward political mobility. Even for elected officeholders, the official's only real constituency is his boss—his principal patron within the multilayered clientage structure. It is that person who will determine the officeholder's next position within the system. In the case of members of Congress, the effects of the *camarilla* system are reinforced by the prohibition on immediate reelection which was introduced into the constitution in 1933. Members of the Senate and Chamber of Deputies must skip at least one term before they can run again for a congressional seat. Under this system, it is the president and his closest political aides who decide where members of Congress will go after their terms expire—not their nominal constituents.

When a *camarilla* leader moves vertically or horizontally within the political system, the key members of his team move with him. For example, Carlos Salinas followed his boss, Miguel de la Madrid, from the Treasury Ministry to the Ministry of Planning and Budget, when de la Madrid was promoted to cabinet rank. Joining

TABLE 2
CAREER OF ERNESTO ZEDILLO PONCE DE LEÓN

1951: **Born in Mexico City**
Raised in Mexicali, Baja California, in a lower-middle-class family (father was an electrician and later a small building contractor; mother was a secretary).

1965–1972: **College preparatory and undergraduate studies at IPN (National Polytechnic Institute), Mexico City**
Majored in economics.

1971–1974: **Researcher in the Office of the Presidency**
Conducted studies in the Division of Economic and Social Planning, under economist Leopoldo Solís.

1973: **Postgraduate study abroad**
Training in evaluation of human capital investment projects at Bradford University, England.

1973–1974: **Teaching at National Polytechnic Institute, Mexico City**
Taught basic economics courses.

1974–1978: **Postgraduate study at Yale University**
Completed M.A. and Ph.D. programs, with a doctoral dissertation on management of "External Public Indebtedness in Mexico."

1978–1987: **Work in Banco de México (central bank)**
Held positions as staff economist, assistant manager of economic and financial research, and director of FICORCA (trust fund that bailed out private Mexican businesses whose debts threatened their survival during the economic crisis of the 1980s).

1987–1992: **Ministry of Planning and Budget (SPP)**
Appointed undersecretary of planning and budget control by SPP Secretary Carlos Salinas de Gortari. Promoted to secretary of SPP when Salinas became president in 1988. (This cabinet post was eliminated in 1992 when Salinas merged SPP into a newly expanded Finance Ministry, headed by Pedro Aspe, a leading contender for the presidency in 1994.)

1992–1993: **Secretary of Public Education**
Appointed by Salinas to this post as a consolation prize, since there was no more room in the economic cabinet.

1993–1994: **Institutional Revolutionary Party (PRI)**
Campaign manager for PRI presidential candidate Luis Donaldo Colosio, until his assassination on March 23, 1994; selected by Salinas to replace Colosio as PRI presidential candidate; elected August 21, 1994.

1994–2000: **President of Mexico**

the "wrong" *camarilla* can entail high career costs, but it is not necessarily fatal to one's long-term political prospects. All successful political leaders in Mexico are associated with multiple *camarillas* at different points in their careers.[18] It is acceptable to shift loyalties when the upward mobility of one's political mentor has been blocked. Politically agile individuals who have built personal alliances with some members of a rival *camarilla* can often jump directly from a losing *camarilla* to the winning one.

To move steadily up the hierarchy, a person must be concerned not only about joining the "right" *camarilla* but with building one's own. The larger and more diverse the *camarilla*, and the more tentacles it extends into all parts of the government bureaucracy and the PRI, the more powerful its leader is. The strongest *camarillas* built in recent *sexenios* have also linked several different generations of political leaders. This was particularly true of Carlos Salinas's extremely large *camarilla*, which linked him — through family, school, or career ties — to practically every person who had headed an economic cabinet ministry since the 1940s.[19] He had built alliances with many members of the traditional PRIista political class as well as technocrats in the government bureaucracy.

Mexico's most recent president, Ernesto Zedillo, is a conspicuous exception to this pattern of career building. When he became the PRI's presidential nominee in 1994, Zedillo's *camarilla* was very small and narrow by modern standards — some would say precisely because he never intended to become president. This "accidental" president was considered, as late as November 1993, a dark-horse candidate for the presidency. He had spent most of his career within the central bank and the Ministry of Planning and Budget (see table 2). He had very few contacts with career politicians or officials in the "political" ministries of the federal government. In fact, he apparently had only a single senior adviser on strictly political issues prior to his selection by Carlos Salinas as a presidential candidate. In choosing his cabinet and senior aides, Zedillo had to draw heavily on holdovers from the Salinas administration; only three could be considered 100 percent Zedillistas. Now that he is in office, Zedillo's lack of extensive *camarilla* alliances of his own making could be either an asset or a liability. On the one hand, he owes political debts to very few and

---

[18]See Roderic A. Camp, "Camarillas in Mexican Politics: The Case of the Salinas Cabinet," *Mexican Studies* 6:1 (Winter 1990), pp. 85–107.

[19]Miguel Angel Centeno and Jeffrey Weldon, "A Small Circle of Friends: Elite Survival in Mexico," paper presented at the International Congress of the Latin American Studies Association, Washington, D.C., April 1991. See also Centeno, *Democracy within Reason*, pp. 163–71.

thus should have greater room for maneuver; on the other, his support base may be too narrow to sustain the harsh austerity policies and disruptive political changes that he has begun to implement.

Recruiting the Political Elite

What kinds of people gain entry into Mexico's national political elite, and who makes it to the top? At least since the days of the Porfiriato, the Mexican political elite has been recruited predominantly from the middle class. The 1910 revolution did not open up the political elite to large numbers of people from peasant or urban laborer backgrounds. That opening occurred only in the 1930s, during the Cárdenas administration, and then mainly at the local and state levels rather than among the national-level elite. By 1989, only 8.3 percent of all state governors, senators, and cabinet and subcabinet members had peasant or working-class origins; in a sample of 1,113 federal government bureaucrats, only 0.7 percent said that their fathers were peasants while 0.9 percent described them as workers.[1]

In recent *sexenios*, the national political elite has become more homogeneous in several important ways. As pointed out above, its members have been drawn increasingly from the ranks of *capitalinos*—people born or raised in Mexico City. By the 1980s more than half of the presidential cabinet had been born in Mexico City, and an even higher percentage had been raised there.[2] Postgraduate education, especially at elite foreign universities and in disciplines like economics and public administration, has become much more important as a ticket of entry into the national political elite. Over half of the cabinet members appointed by Presidents de la Madrid, Salinas, and Zedillo had studied economics or administration, and over half of those who received training in these subjects at the graduate level did so in the United States. The economic cabinets of Mexico's three most recent presidents have been filled with recipients of Ph.D. degrees from universities such as Harvard, MIT, Stanford, Yale, and Chicago.

---

[1]Centeno, *Democracy within Reason*, p. 112.
[2]Ibid.

How should we interpret this trend in elite recruitment? According to one careful analysis,

> The government did not necessarily need [professional] economists to make policy. Rather, a cohesive group inside the state first established their dominance and *then* utilized supposedly meritocratic criteria to benefit those with whom they shared key attributes. . . . The elite's faith in the rationality of economics not only helped determine the kinds of policies adopted by it but also served to exclude rival claims of knowledge. These educational qualifications further increase the social exclusivity and homogeneity of the ruling elite by requiring financial and professional commitments to education that only a select few can make.[3]

The economic debacles of the 1980s and 1990s in Mexico are a powerful reminder that expertise in the discipline of economics, in the hands of Mexico's bureaucratic elite, need not translate into sound public policy.

Since the 1970s, kinship ties have also become more important as a common denominator of those who attain top positions of political power. Increasingly, such people are born into politically prominent families that have already produced state governors, cabinet ministers, federal legislators, and even presidents. And these political families are increasingly interconnected: At least one-third of the government officials and politicians interviewed by one researcher for several books on the Mexican political elite were related to other officials, not counting those related through marriage and the traditional rite of *compadrazgo* (becoming a godparent to a friend's child).[4] Family connections can give an aspiring political leader a powerful advantage over rivals. In effect, he inherits the *camarilla* that has been assembled by his politically prominent relative, and the relative himself becomes a key mentor and opener of doors.

The growing importance of kinship ties, postgraduate education in certain fields, and other indicators of increasing homogeneity in personal backgrounds has caused some observers to worry that Mexico's political elite is becoming more closed and

---

[3]Ibid., pp. 121–22.

[4]Unpublished data from Roderic A. Camp, Center for Latin American Studies, Tulane University. See Camp, "Family Relationships in Mexican Politics," *Journal of Politics* 44 (August 1982), pp. 848–62; and Smith, *Labyrinths of Power*, pp. 307–10.

inbred. While its social base may, indeed, be narrowing, the modern Mexican political elite still shows considerable fluidity; the massive turnover of officeholders every six years is proof of that. The circulation of political elites in Mexico is not just a game of musical chairs. According to one study, 80 percent of the top 200 officeholders are replaced every 12 years, and 90 percent every 18 years. At the end of each administration, nearly one-third of the top-level players actually drop out of political life.[5] This helps to explain why in Mexico, unlike other postrevolutionary countries such as China and (until recently) the Soviet Union, the regime has not become a gerontocracy. In fact, the median age of cabinet members and presidential aspirants in Mexico has been dropping; in recent *sexenios*, most have been in their late 30s or early 40s.

The movement of thousands of persons into and out of the ruling elite at regular intervals has been an important source of political stability in Mexico since the 1930s, because it reinforced the idea of "giving everyone a turn." At least at the highest levels of the system, members of the political elite remained in power for only a certain length of time. The implied lesson was that politically ambitious individuals would get their chance to acquire power, status, and wealth—if they were patient, persistent, and self-disciplined.

In recent decades this calculus of expectations has been upset by the rise of the so-called *técnicos*. Beginning with the Echeverría presidency in the 1970s and continuing through the de la Madrid, Salinas, and Zedillo *sexenios*, persons whose careers have been built mainly in the arena of electoral politics in the Congress and in the labor unions and peasant organizations affiliated with the ruling party have been eclipsed in the competition for high office. They have lost out increasingly to technocrats whose main ticket of admission to the national political elite is an advanced university degree (together with the right family and *camarilla* ties). Typically, the *técnicos* spend their entire career within the government bureaucracy, especially the financial and planning agencies. They generally lack substantial personal constituencies outside the bureaucracy, because they have not had the opportunity nor the need to develop such followings.

The vast majority of technocrats who make it to the highest levels of the system today have not run for elective office. Ernesto Zedillo is the fifth man in a row to become president of Mexico without having held any previous elective office. The most upwardly mobile *técnicos* typically get their only direct experience in party politics by helping to run the presidential campaign of the

---

[5]Smith, *Labyrinths of Power*, chap. 6.

man in whose administration they hope to serve. If he had lived to become president, Luis Donaldo Colosio would have been exceptional—a technocrat (with a master's degree in regional planning from the University of Pennsylvania) who had served in the Congress and as titular head of the PRI (president of the party's Central Executive Council) during the first half of the Salinas administration.

Técnicos rise to power far more rapidly than the average traditional politician. Carlos Salinas, for example, was only 34 years old when he was appointed to a cabinet post by President de la Madrid, and 39 when he was nominated for the presidency. The so-called traditional *políticos* are conspicuously older when they attain positions of power, because they usually have spent many years doing service for the PRI and/or its affiliated organizations.[6]

With the rise of the technocrats, traditional politicians have found their access to the most important posts in the government blocked. Career politicians must now implement decisions made by technocrats, who are far more preoccupied with economic reforms and economic problem solving than with maintaining the comfortable arrangements that traditional politicians have fashioned for themselves. Old-line *políticos* have been increasingly alarmed by the technocrats' efforts to change the rules of the electoral game, in ways that make it more difficult for the *políticos* to do their jobs and to retain their traditional share of public positions. The PRI's old guard—the most retrograde of whom are commonly referred to as *los dinosaurios*—have opposed increases in genuine electoral competition, while some high-ranking technocrats—including, initially, Presidents de la Madrid and Salinas—pushed for "modernization" of the PRI and the electoral system, if only to keep the PRI in power without recourse to massive fraud.

The resulting tensions contributed importantly to the breakdown in PRI unity that occurred in 1987–1988, which gave rise to the dissident candidacy of Cuauhtémoc Cárdenas and the creation of the PRD. Through his cabinet appointments (a blend of card-carrying young technocrats and older, seasoned politicians) and his go-slow approach to political reform, President Salinas succeeded in reducing tensions within the national political elite, but only temporarily. The types of basic changes in the system now being advocated by Ernesto Zedillo are much more threatening to

---

[6]On the widening generational gap within Mexico's political elite, see Peter H. Smith, "Leadership and Change: Intellectuals and Technocrats in Mexico," in Roderic A. Camp, ed., *Mexico's Political Stability: The Next Five Years* (Boulder, Colo.: Westview, 1986), pp. 101–17.

the interests of the traditional political class than anything ever contemplated by the Salinistas.

The dichotomy between *técnicos* and *políticos* is frequently overdrawn. The technocrats have been stereotyped as "number crunchers" whose abstract formulas for public policy ignore popular needs and frustrations, and who lack basic political skills. Ernesto Zedillo's inept handling of a controversy over publication of a new series of "revisionist" history textbooks for the country's elementary schools, during his brief tenure as President Salinas's secretary of education, was widely cited as an example of the technocrats' political skill deficit.[7] While many high-ranking technocrats could fairly be criticized for insensitivity to social realities, those who rise to the top of the government hierarchy today could not possibly achieve such positions by technical competence and administrative experience alone; they must be accomplished political alliance builders as well. Their bureaucratic responsibilities, as well as the often brutal competition with other technocrats aspiring to higher office, require them to develop such skills, or be knocked out of the game.

---

[7]See, for example, "The Textbook Controversy (Part Two): Zedillo's Bungle," *Mexico and NAFTA Regional Report* (London), RM-93-09, September 23, 1994, p. 3.

Interest Representation and Political Control

In Mexico's presidentialist system, important public policies usually have been initiated and shaped by the inner circle of presidential advisers before they were even presented for public discussion. Thus, most effective interest representation took place within the upper levels of the government bureaucracy. The structures that aggregate and articulate interests in Western democracies (the ruling political party, labor unions, and so on) actually served other purposes in the Mexican system: limiting the scope of citizens' demands on the government, mobilizing electoral support for the regime, helping to legitimate it in the eyes of other countries, distributing jobs and other material rewards to select individuals and groups.

Since the late 1930s, Mexico has had a corporatist system of interest representation in which each citizen and societal segment should relate to the state through a single structure "licensed" by the state to organize and represent that sector of society (peasants, urban unionized workers, businesspeople, teachers, and so on). The official party itself was divided into three sectors: the labor sector, the peasant sector, and the popular sector, a catchall representing various segments of the middle class (government employees, other white-collar workers, small merchants, private landowners) and residents of low-income urban neighborhoods. Each sector has been dominated by one mass organization; other organizations are affiliated with each party sector, but their influence is dwarfed by that of the "peak" organization. Thus, the labor sector has been dominated by the Confederación de Trabajadores de México (CTM); the peasant sector by the Confederación Nacional Campesina (CNC); and the popular sector by the Confederación Nacional de Organizaciones Populares (CNOP).

A number of powerful organized interest groups—foreign and domestic entrepreneurs, the military, the Catholic Church—are not formally represented in the PRI. These groups deal directly with the governmental elite, often at the presidential or cabinet level; they do not need the PRI to make their preferences known. They also have well-placed representatives within the executive branch who can be counted on to articulate their interests. In addition, the business community is organized into several government-chartered confederations that take positions on public issues and have their preferences widely disseminated through the mass media. Since the Cárdenas administration, all but a small minority of the country's industrialists and businesspeople have been required by law to join one of these employers' organizations. In the 1980s, several business organizations independent of the state-sanctioned associations (especially the Confederación Patronal de la República Mexicana, COPARMEX, and the Consejo Coordinador Empresarial, CCE) assumed leading roles in criticizing government economic policies.

Because the ruling party and the national legislature do not effectively aggregate interests in the Mexican system, individuals and groups seeking something from the government often circumvent their nominal representatives in the PRI sectoral organizations and the Congress, and seek satisfaction of their needs through personal contacts—patrons—within the government bureaucracy. These patron-client relationships compartmentalize the society into discrete, noninteracting, vertical segments that serve as pillars of the regime. Within the lower class, for example, unionized urban workers are separated from nonunion urban workers; *ejidatarios* from small private landholders and landless agricultural workers. The middle class is compartmentalized into government bureaucrats, educators, health care professionals, lawyers, economists, and so forth. Thus, competition *between* social classes is replaced by highly fragmented competition *within* classes.

The articulation of interests through patron-client networks assists the regime by fragmenting popular demands into small-scale, highly individualized or localized requests that can be granted or denied case by case. Officials are rarely confronted with collective demands from broad social groupings. Rather than having to act on a request from a whole category of people (slum dwellers, *ejidatarios*, teachers), they have easier, less costly choices to make (as between competing petitions from several neighborhoods for a paved street or a piped water system). The clientelistic structure thus provides a mechanism for distributing public services and other benefits in a highly selective, discretionary if not arbitrary manner. It puts the onus on potential beneficiaries to identify and cultivate the "right" patrons within the government bureaucracy, while making it more difficult for dissident leaders to organize people on the basis of broadly shared economic grievances.[1]

The appearance in recent years of independent citizens' organizations not tied into the regime's clientelistic networks has introduced new complexity and uncertainty into the political system. Numerous movements and organizations have emerged spontaneously among the urban poor, peasants, and even some middle-class groups like schoolteachers and private agricultural producers, which the PRI-government apparatus has generally failed to incorporate.[2] These movements developed partly in response to the economic crises of the 1980s and 1990s, partly because of the declining responsiveness of existing state-chartered "mass" organizations to popular demands, and partly as a result of general societal modernization (expansion of mass communications, higher education levels, urbanization, changes in occupational structure, and the like). The attractiveness of independent popular movements also reflects the disdain with which the entrenched, state-affiliated organizations are now regarded. The PRI's sectoral organizations are viewed by most Mexicans as corrupt, manipulative, self-serving extensions of the state bureaucracy that provide no effective representation of their interests.

After the dismal performance of the sectoral organizations in delivering votes to Carlos Salinas in the 1988 presidential election, the dysfunctional nature of the corporatist system of interest representation became a matter of urgent concern. The newly installed head of the official party, Luis Donaldo Colosio, saw a need to change "the basic terms of the relationship between the PRI and its mass base. Workers' votes are influenced more by the problems in their immediate environment; by their lives outside the workplace. The lack of water, sewerage, and other services; crime; deficient schools—that's what concerns them. The votes for the PRI are not in the [sectoral] organizations, but in the homes of the workers."[3] Thus, Colosio, his boss President Salinas, and like-minded "political modernizers" in the PRI-government apparatus

[1]See Evelyn P. Stevens, *Protest and Response in Mexico* (Cambridge, Mass.: MIT Press, 1974), p. 94.

[2]See Foweraker and Craig, eds., *Popular Movements and Political Change in Mexico*; Neil Harvey, *The New Agrarian Movement in Mexico, 1979–1990* (London: Institute of Latin American Studies, Monograph No. 23, 1990); and Joe Foweraker, *Popular Mobilization in Mexico: The Teachers' Movement, 1977–87* (Cambridge and New York: Cambridge University Press, 1993; distributed by the Center for U.S.-Mexican Studies, University of California, San Diego).

[3]Interview with the author, January 17, 1989, quoted in Cornelius, Gentleman, and Smith, eds., *Mexico's Alternative Political Futures*, p. 28.

sought to de-emphasize, if not eliminate, the role of discredited *sectores* in interest articulation and aggregation. They decided that ossified corporatist structures should be replaced gradually with territorially based "movements" and committees, led by new cadres who could distance themselves (and, implicitly, the PRI itself) from the detested party bosses who ran the sectoral organizations and foster a more direct relationship between the PRI and individual citizens.

During the Salinas *sexenio*, the drive to establish a new kind of connection between the ruling party and its mass base took two principal forms. First, several attempts were made to reorganize the party's popular sector along territorial lines and install new leaders. In 1993 the CNOP was renamed the Frente Nacional de Organizaciones y Ciudadanos (FNOC), but the popular sector's traditional corporatist structure was essentially reaffirmed. This outcome represented a victory for the "dinosaurs" within the popular sector, who accurately perceived the proposed focus on the local community rather than the workplace as a threat to their fiefdoms.[4]

Second, through the National Solidarity Program (PRO-NASOL), the Salinas administration created what amounted to a parallel structure of interest representation that was very much territorially based and not at all dependent on the PRI's sectors. The more than 150,000 Solidarity Committees established in less than five years in low-income urban neighborhoods and rural communities throughout the country were more than a mechanism for rebuilding electoral support for the PRI by demonstrating that the system could respond more rapidly to citizen demands for services and urban infrastructure. In President Salinas's grand design, they were also intended to transform state-society relations, build alliances with (or incorporate) the independent popular movements that had emerged in the previous two decades, and serve as a recruiting and training ground for new-style political leaders.[5] After analyses of the 1991 midterm elections showed that the Solidarity program contributed significantly to the PRI's impressive recovery in those elections, it was believed that Salinas might try to use the local Solidarity Committees as the framework for a new political party or a radically reformed PRI. But this idea—if it was ever seriously considered—was never implemented. Resistance from entrenched leaders of the PRI's *sectores* was too strong,

---

[4]See Nikki Craske, "Corporatism Revisited: Salinas and the Reform of the Popular Sector," Institute of Latin American Studies, University of London, Research Paper No. 37 (1994), pp. 21–24.

[5]See Cornelius, Craig, and Fox, eds., *Transforming State-Society Relations in Mexico*, p. 19.

and even the Salinista reformers may have thought that the risks inherent in dismantling traditional corporatism were too high.[6]

Unquestionably, the Mexican regime's vaunted political control capabilities have been weakened by the economic and political crises of recent *sexenios*. Nevertheless, the traditional instruments of control—patron-client relationships, *caciquismo* (local-level boss rule), the captive labor movement, selective repression of dissidents by government security forces—remain in place and have not lost all of their former effectiveness. The remarkably low incidence of protest behavior, unauthorized strikes, and other forms of civil disobedience in Mexico during the economic crisis of the 1980s suggests that the PRI-government apparatus remained highly adept at dividing, buying off, co-opting, and—if necessary—repressing protest movements before they get out of hand. While protest behavior of all sorts has become much more common in the 1990s, fear of government repression remains high. In a national opinion survey conducted in the summer of 1994, 55 percent of the respondents agreed with the statement that "people in Mexico are afraid to express what they think about politics and government"; only 38 percent said that Mexicans felt free to express their views.[7]

The PRI-government apparatus has also been remarkably successful in using the mass media to maintain political control. Although the government does not directly censor the media, there can be significant economic penalties for engaging in criticism or investigative reporting that seriously embarrasses the president. For example, government advertising—a major source of revenue for most newspapers and magazines—can be withheld from offending publications. While the Salinas administration ended the long-standing practices of bribing reporters to get favorable treatment and threatening to cut off newsprint to troublesome periodicals, by 1995 only three Mexico City newspapers and a handful of dissident news magazines were vigorously, dependably critical of government policies and performance.

Whatever they say about a president or his administration, the print media reach only a tiny fraction of the Mexican population (even the largest Mexico City newspapers are believed to have circulations under 100,000). Television is the main source of political information for the vast majority of Mexicans, and it is virtually monopolized by a huge private firm, Televisa, which has a notoriously close working relationship with the PRI-government apparatus. While dissenting opinions are heard with increasing frequency on radio talk shows,

---

[6]See Craske, "Corporatism Revisited," pp. 26–32.

[7]Belden & Russonello y Ciencia Aplicada, "Resumen de una encuesta sobre preferencias electorales en México," *Este País* 44 (November 1994), special supplement, p. 7.

the owners of radio stations must live under constant threat that their licenses to broadcast can be suspended if commentators are overly critical. Very few owners are willing to risk the personal financial consequences of completely unfettered political speech.

PARTIDO REVOLUCIONARIO INSTITUCIONAL (PRI)

Mexico's "official" party, the Partido Revolucionario Institucional, was founded in 1929 by President Plutarco Elías Calles to serve as a mechanism for reducing violent conflict among contenders for public office and for consolidating the power of the central government, at the expense of the personalistic, local, and state-level political machines that had passed for political parties during the decade following the 1910–1920 revolution. Between 1920 and 1929, there had been four major rebellions against the central executive by these subnational political machines. As historian Lorenzo Meyer has observed, the official party was a party born not to fight for power, nor to share it with the opposition, but rather to *administer* it.[8]

For more than half a century the ruling party served with impressive efficiency, as a mechanism for resolving elite conflicts, for co-opting newly emerging interest groups into the system, and for legitimating the regime through the electoral process. Potential defectors from the official party were deterred by the government's manipulation of electoral rules, which made it virtually impossible for any dissident faction to bolt the party *and* win an election. Dissident movements did emerge occasionally, but before the neo-Cardenista coalition contested the 1988 election, no breakaway presidential candidacy had been able to garner more than 16 percent of the vote (by official count).

In 1938 President Lázaro Cárdenas transformed the official party from a mechanism for elite conflict resolution and co-optation into a mass-based political party that could be used explicitly to build popular support for government policies and mobilize participation in elections. Cárdenas accomplished this by merging into the official party the local-, state-, and national-level organizations of peasants and urban workers that had been created during his presidency.[9] This reorganization established the party's claim to be an inclusionary party—one that would seek to absorb into it as many as possible

---

[8]Lorenzo Meyer, "La democracia política: esperando a Godot," *Nexos* 100 (April 1986), p. 42. See also Meyer, "Democratization of the PRI: Mission Impossible?" in Cornelius, Gentleman, and Smith, eds., *Mexico's Alternative Political Futures*, pp. 325–48.

[9]This process is described in Wayne A. Cornelius, "Nation-building, Participation, and Distribution: The Politics of Social Reform under Cárdenas," in Gabriel A. Almond et al., *Crisis, Choice, and Change: Historical Studies of Political Development* (Boston: Little, Brown, 1973), pp. 392–498.

of the diverse economic interests and political tendencies that were represented in Mexican society. The official party and its affiliated mass organizations occupied so much political space that opposition parties and movements found it difficult to recruit supporters.

From the beginning, the official party was an appendage of the government itself, especially of the presidency. It was never a truly independent arena of political competition. A handful of nationally powerful party leaders, such as Fidel Velázquez, patriarch of the PRI-affiliated labor movement, occasionally constrained government actions, but the official party itself has never determined the basic directions of government economic and social policies. Indeed, one of the key factors underlying the erosion of party unity and discipline in the late 1980s and the PRI's overwhelming defeats in state-level elections beginning in 1995 was the party's inability to distance itself from unpopular austerity policies made by technocrats in the federal government.

During the 1940s and 1950s Mexico's ruling party became one of the world's most accomplished vote-getting machines, guaranteeing an overwhelming victory at the polls for all but a handful of its candidates in every election. None of the party's nominees for president has ever been officially defeated (though the claimed victories of Manuel Avila Camacho in 1940 and Carlos Salinas in 1988 have been questioned by numerous analysts), and until 1988–1989 none of its candidates for federal senator or state governor had been denied victory. Only since the 1970s have opposition parties been able to win appreciable numbers of municipal presidencies and seats in the federal legislature.

The official party has always had a number of powerful advantages over its electoral competitors. Privileged access to the mass media (and particularly, since the 1960s, television) is one of them. Electoral law reforms in the 1990s expanded the opposition parties' access to the media, but coverage remains highly unequal. As mentioned above, television pays as little attention as possible to the campaigns of opposition candidates. Newspaper coverage is only slightly more balanced. In 1994, the five principal newspapers in Mexico City devoted, on average, 40.8 percent of their space for coverage of the national election campaigns to the PRI, 11.6 percent to the PAN, and 17.8 percent to the PRD; the remainder was allocated to the six other, minor parties that competed in the 1994 elections.[10] At the state level, the imbalance is often much worse. For example, independent studies of coverage of the hotly contested 1995 gubernatorial campaign in Yucatán found that the

---

[10]Raúl Trejo Delarbre, "1994: El voto de la prensa," *Nexos* 204 (December 1994), pp. 16–19.

state's mass media favored the PRI over the opposition parties by as much as 9 to 1.

The official party traditionally has enjoyed virtually unlimited access to government funds to finance its campaigns, in addition to "dues" automatically deducted from the salaries of government employees. No one knew how much was actually being transferred from government coffers to the PRI, since Mexico had no laws requiring the reporting of campaign income and expenditures. However, when the PANista government took power in the state of Baja California, it found bank and legal records showing that more than $10 million in government funds had been channeled to the PRI for its 1989 gubernatorial campaign in that state. Reforms to the federal electoral code in 1993 and 1994 established minimal public reporting requirements for campaign income and expenditures, as well as Mexico's first-ever limits on individual and corporate contributions to electoral campaigns.

There are strong indications that the Zedillo administration has ended direct government subsidization of PRI operations. However, in the 1993–1994 electoral code reforms, ceilings on private contributions were set very high—the equivalent of $650,000 for an individual contribution, as compared with a maximum of $20,000 allowable under U.S. election laws. With its privileged access to financing from the private sector, the PRI could continue to outspend its opponents by a huge margin, even without cash from government sources. In 1994, the PRI could legally spend $44 million on its presidential campaign, and its capacity to shake down big business owners for contributions remained undiminished. Indeed, the PRI had more money to spend on its campaigns, at all levels, than ever before, *despite* the contribution limits included in the newest electoral code. In the same year, the PRI candidate for governor in the state of Tabasco spent in excess of $50 million on his campaign—many times the legal limit for a gubernatorial race. This abuse came to light only after the defeated PRD candidate was able to produce massive, incontrovertible evidence.

Moreover, a new prohibition on "the use of public resources and programs to benefit any political party or electoral campaign" may be exceedingly difficult to enforce; such are the privileges of incumbency enjoyed by ruling parties everywhere. In some states, PRIista governors openly use public resources under their control to promote PRI candidates for state and local offices, brushing off criticism from opposition parties. Not surprisingly, the opposition parties are pressing for yet another round of federal electoral law reforms, aimed particularly at leveling the playing field in the areas of campaign finance and media access.

As the party in power, the PRI has benefited from a vast network of government patronage, through which small-scale material benefits could be delivered to large segments of the population. Government austerity induced by the economic crisis of the 1980s sharply reduced the resources that could be pumped through that national patronage system. However, during the Salinas *sexenio*, the National Solidarity Program delivered more than $15 billion in benefits to some 25 million Mexicans. The benefits ranged from refurbished schoolrooms and scholarships to keep low-income children in school, to health clinics, paved streets, potable water and sewage systems, housing, and support for small-business development.[11] These small-scale investments were especially visible in the vote-rich urban slums, where the Cardenista coalition won much of its support in 1988. In the 1991 congressional elections, individuals who had personally benefited from the Solidarity program were strongly disposed to vote for PRI candidates.[12] In 1994, just in time for national elections, the government also launched PROCAMPO, a program offering direct cash payments to millions of subsistence farmers. Some 2.8 million PROCAMPO checks were delivered to beneficiaries in the two months preceding the August 21 elections. The opposition parties complained bitterly about the utilization of Solidarity and PRO-CAMPO funds to boost PRI candidates, but they could not deny the popularity of these new pork-barrel programs. The results of some quantitative studies suggest that the Solidarity program was, in fact, used strategically by the PRI-government apparatus as an asset in the electoral arena.[13]

The PRI is the only political party in Mexico that possesses a truly nationwide network of campaign organizers, neighborhood vote promoters, and poll watchers. The PRI's unmatched mobilizational capacity was demonstrated anew in 1994, when it was able to put more than 1.2 million party militants into the field on election day and during the weeks immediately preceding it. The huge size and geographic dispersion of the ruling party's network of militants translate into great advantages at election time. For example, it requires nearly 100,000 poll watchers to cover every polling place

---

[11]For a detailed breakdown of the numerous Solidarity subprograms, see John Bailey and Jennifer Boone, "National Solidarity: A Summary of Program Elements," in Cornelius, Craig, and Fox, eds., *Transforming State-Society Relations in Mexico*, pp. 329–38. See also, José Luis Piñeyro and Gabriela Barajas, "Seguridad nacional y pobreza en México: notas sobre el Pronasol," *El Cotidiano* 71 (September 1995), pp. 78–85.

[12]Alejandro Moreno, "Agosto de 1991: ¿Por qué se votó por el PRI?" *Este País* 33 (December 1993), pp. 26–28.

[13]See Cornelius, Craig, and Fox, eds., *Transforming State-Society Relations in Mexico*, chaps. 7 and 12.

in the country during a presidential election. For the 1994 national elections, the PRI had representatives stationed at 99.5 percent of the polling places; the PRD covered 80.5 percent; the PAN, 75.7 percent.[14]

Historically, the official party's most potent advantage over the competition has been its ability to commit electoral fraud with relative impunity. A wide variety of techniques have been used: stuffing ballot boxes; intimidating potential opposition supporters by threatening to deny or withdraw government benefits; disqualifying opposition party poll watchers; relocating polling places at the last minute to sites known only to PRI supporters; manipulating voter registration lists, padding them with nonexistent or nonresident PRIistas, and/or *rasurando* ("shaving off") those who might vote for opposition parties; issuing multiple voting credentials to PRI supporters; organizing *carruseles* ("flying brigades") of PRI supporters who were transported by truck or van to vote at several different polling places; and so forth. Moreover, with majority representation in all the local, state, and national government entities that controlled vote counting, the PRI could rely on these bodies to manipulate the tallies to deny victory to opposition candidates or, if necessary, to nullify unfavorable election outcomes. Final results often were negotiated by federal election authorities with leaders of the opposition parties.

Adding votes to the PRI column, rather than taking them away from opposition parties, has been the most common form of electoral fraud. In some predominantly rural districts, this practice led to election results in which the number of votes credited to the PRI candidate exceeded the total number of registered voters, or even the total number of adults estimated from the most recent population census. Such was the case in the 1988 and 1991 elections held in the Ocosingo district of Chiapas—the epicenter of the Zapatista rebellion of 1994–1995.

In a successful effort to build domestic and international credibility for the 1994 national elections, the Salinas government introduced a number of important safeguards against fraud. New, high-tech, photo-identification voter credentials were issued to virtually the entire 42.5 million–member electorate. The Federal Electoral Institute (IFE) was greatly strengthened and given considerable autonomy. Its key decision-making body was made independent of control by PRI and government representatives. Beginning in May 1994, six independent "citizen magistrates," whose appointments had to be approved by two-thirds of the

---

[14]Statistics calculated from Instituto Federal Electoral, *1994: Tu elección—memoria del proceso electoral federal* (México, D.F.: IFE, 1995), tables 6.4a and 6.4b, pp. 307–08.

Consejeros Ciudadanos (independent "Citizen Magistrates") debate a motion during a meeting of the newly reconstituted executive council of the Federal Electoral Institute (IFE) in July 1994. For the first time in Mexican history, the entity responsible for the conduct of national elections was not controlled by representatives of the government and the ruling party. Source: Imagenlatina-Angeles Torrejón; by permission of Secretaría de Gobernación, Mexico.

Congress (thus requiring them to have the support of at least one of the opposition parties), had control of the IFE's revamped, eleven-member executive council. A new system of independent electoral tribunals was established to adjudicate election disputes, and a special prosecutor's office was established to investigate alleged violations of the electoral laws. A broad range of offenses—not previously subject to prosecution—were defined as electoral crimes. The role of independent, Mexican citizen observers in monitoring the casting and tallying of votes was formally recognized, and the presence of foreign election observers (euphemistically termed "international visitors") was legitimated. (The Federal Electoral Institute accredited some 81,620 Mexican citizens plus more than 500 foreign "visitors" as observers of the August 21, 1994, national election.) Exit polls of voters and "quick counts" of the actual vote by the IFE as well as by private organizations were authorized and publicly announced on election night.

Taken together, these innovations, which cost the Salinas government more than $1 billion, represent a major advance toward improving the security, professionalism, and fairness of the Mexican electoral system. The 1994 elections, which brought a record 78 percent of the potential electorate to the polls, demon-

President-to-be Ernesto Zedillo casts his ballot in the August 21, 1994, election.
Source: *Instituto Federal Electoral, Mexico.*

strated that under the new system it is possible to conduct relatively clean and credible elections in much of urban Mexico.
However, various types of irregularities—especially violations of
ballot secrecy and efforts by local bosses to induce voters to
support the PRI—were still widespread in the more isolated, rural
areas.[15] Subsequent state and local elections in various parts of the
country have demonstrated that subnational PRI leaders continue
to use direct threats and other forms of intimidation, particularly
against peasant voters.

---

[15]The largest, independent election observation network operating in 1994 reached
the following conclusion about the aggregate impact of the election's irregularities:
"The quantitative impact of [the documented irregularities] cannot be calculated
with certainty and precision. It is likely that they did not alter the outcome of the
presidential election. Nevertheless, they did alter the . . . composition of the
Chamber of Deputies, and possibly that of the Senate" (Alianza Cívica/Observación
1994, "La calidad de la jornada electoral del 21 de agosto de 1994," México, D.F.,
September 19, 1994, p. 16). See also Sergio Aguayo Quezada, "A Mexican Milestone," *Journal of Democracy* 6:2 (April 1995), pp. 157–67; and Jonathan Fox, "National
Electoral Choices in Rural Mexico," paper presented at the conference on "The
Reform of the Mexican Agrarian Reform," Columbia University, New York, April
1995.

The share of the vote claimed by the PRI has been declining for nearly 30 years, but until recently the erosion has been gradual and has not threatened the party's grasp on the presidency and state governorships (see figure 2). The proportion of electoral districts dominated by the PRI (see the first three columns of table 3) has dropped dramatically, from 84.5 percent in 1964 to 10.6 percent in 1994. In the 1994 federal elections, the PRI faced significant competition from at least two opposition parties in more than half of the country's electoral districts (see table 3, "multiparty competition"). Outright majority victories by opposition candidates for congressional seats remain relatively rare (the opposition parties' presence in the Congress has expanded mainly because of the proportional representation system created through several sets of electoral law reforms); but the Mexican electoral system as a whole has become much more competitive in the last 15 years. At the state level, the PRI's vote share in 1994 ranged from just above 40 percent to just below 60 percent. In the same year, PRI support topped 70 percent in just 7 of the country's 300 electoral districts, compared with 75 in the 1991 elections.[16] The "Soviet-style" precincts that regularly delivered 98 to 100 percent of their votes to PRI candidates have largely disappeared.[17]

One of the key factors accounting for the long-term decline in the official party's effectiveness as a vote-getting machine is the massive shift of population from rural to urban areas that has occurred in Mexico since 1950. In that year, 57 percent of the population lived in isolated rural communities of fewer than 2,500 inhabitants; by 1990 less than 29 percent lived in such localities. This massive rural-to-urban migration is reflected in occupational statistics: During the last four decades, the proportion of Mexico's economically active population employed in agriculture dropped from 58.3 to 26.8 percent.

In urban Mexico, authoritarian control mechanisms are less efficacious. Education and income levels are higher, and the middle classes—which provide a considerable share of the opposition vote—are larger. The opposition parties are better organized and have more poll watchers in these places, making it more difficult for the PRI to conceal vote fraud. A smaller proportion of the population is subject to pressures from local-level PRI bosses. The data

---

[16]See Joseph L. Klesner, "The 1994 Mexican Elections: Manifestation of a Divided Society?" *Mexican Studies* 11:1 (Winter 1995), pp. 143–46.

[17]This phenomenon persists, however, in some of Mexico's most underdeveloped states. For example, in local elections held in Chiapas in October 1995, the PRI was credited with all 10,000 votes in the town of Chamula. The PAN received not a single vote in 59 municipalities, and the PRD failed to win a single vote in five municipalities, according to official results.

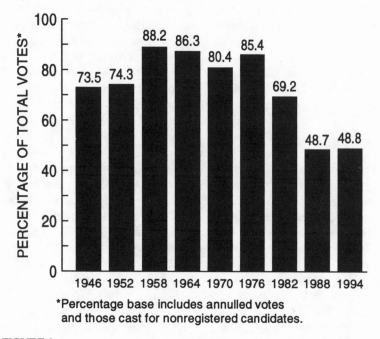

*Percentage base includes annulled votes
and those cast for nonregistered candidates.

FIGURE 2

SUPPORT FOR RULING PARTY'S PRESIDENTIAL CANDIDATE, 1946–1994

Source: Data from the Comisión Federal Electoral, Mexico (for 1946–1988), and from the Instituto Federal Electoral, Mexico (for 1994).

assembled in table 4 reveal that the PRI is significantly weaker in cities with 100,000 or more inhabitants. Support for the PAN is strongest in these urban centers. In the 1988 presidential election, Carlos Salinas, the would-be modernizer of Mexico, derived his margin of victory from the most traditional, underdeveloped parts of the country; he received only one out of four votes cast in Mexico City. Even in rural areas, however, the PRI's formerly safe vote continues to erode. While the PRI still gets a higher share of the vote in rural areas than any other party, in 1994 the average percentage vote for PRI candidates in rural districts fell by 11 percentage points, continuing a trend that began with the 1982 national elections.[18] Moreover, in all states where the PAN won gubernatorial elections in 1995, the party took a large share of the rural vote, for the first time in its history.

[18]See Ann L. Craig and Wayne A. Cornelius, "Houses Divided: Parties and Political Reform in Mexico," in Scott Mainwaring and Timothy R. Scully, eds., *Building Democratic Institutions: Party Systems in Latin America* (Stanford, Calif.: Stanford University Press, 1995), table 8.3, p. 263; and Guadalupe Pacheco Méndez, "El nuevo mapa electoral: dos partidos y medio," *Nexos* 209 (May 1995), pp. 14–17.

TABLE 3
ELECTORAL COMPETITION IN NATIONAL ELECTIONS, 1964–1994
(PERCENTAGE OF 300 FEDERAL ELECTORAL DISTRICTS)

	Type of Competition[a]					
Election Year	PRI Monopoly	Strong PRI Hegemony	Weak PRI Hegemony	Two-party Competition	Multiparty Competition	Opposition Victory
1964	28.1%	52.2%	4.5%	14.0%	—	1.1%
1967	24.2	61.2	3.6	9.7	—	1.2
1970	27.0	53.9	1.7	17.4	—	—
1973	18.7	51.3	4.1	21.8	1.0%	3.1
1976	35.8	44.6	6.7	11.9	0.5	0.5
1979	9.4	48.0	12.3	6.3	22.7	1.3
1982	1.3	51.7	6.3	26.1	14.0	0.3
1985	3.3	41.7	9.0	21.0	21.3	3.7
1988[b]	1.0	19.0	15.0	8.3	34.0	22.7
1991	—	21.7	16.0	18.0	41.0	3.3
1994	—	2.3	8.3	26.0	55.4	8.0

[a]*PRI monopoly* = PRI vote > 95 percent; *strong PRI hegemony* = PRI vote < 95 percent but > 70; *weak PRI hegemony* = PRI vote < 70 percent, but the difference between PRI and second party in district is > 40 percentage points; *two-party competition* = PRI vote < 70 percent, difference between PRI and second party is < 40 percentage points, second party vote > 25 percent, and third party vote < 10 percent; *multiparty competition* = PRI vote < 70, difference between PRI and second party is < 40 percentage points, and second party vote < 25 percent or third-party vote > 10 percent; *opposition victory* = any party's vote > PRI vote.

[b]For 1988, opposition victories include those won by the Cardenista coalition of parties.

Source: Leopoldo Gómez and John Bailey, "La transición política y los dilemas del PRI," *Foro Internacional* 31:1 (July–September 1990), p. 69. Calculations for 1991 and 1994 from Joseph L. Klesner, "The 1994 Mexican Elections: Manifestation of a Divided Society?" *Mexican Studies* 11:1 (Winter 1995), p. 141.

Meanwhile, the urban vote has become more volatile. The PRI lost it badly in the 1985 midterm elections and in the 1988 presidential election; recovered it in the 1991 midterm elections; and held its urban vote share steady in 1994. In Baja California, a state where more than three-quarters of the electorate lives in cities, Cuauhtémoc Cárdenas easily defeated Carlos Salinas in the 1988 presidential election, but in 1989 the same state overwhelmingly elected a PANista as governor.[19] In 1994, the PAN's congressional candidates did poorly in Baja California and the other two states governed at that time by PANistas (Chihuahua and Guanajuato). But in 1995, voters in Baja California and Guanajuato elected PANista governors by decisive margins. Such disparate outcomes reflect the increasingly independent behavior of the Mexican voter. Especially since 1988, a significant minority of Mexicans have been willing to switch party loyalties from one election to the next, to vote for an opposition party in order to

---

[19]See Tonatiuh Guillén López, *Baja California, 1989–1992: alternancia política y transición democrática* (Tijuana, B.C.: El Colegio de la Frontera Norte, 1993); and Rodríguez and Ward, *Political Change in Baja California.*

TABLE 4
PARTY PREFERENCE IN 1994 ELECTIONS, BY AGE, GENDER,
EDUCATION, INCOME LEVEL, AND SIZE OF LOCALITY
(IN PERCENTAGES)

	Party Preference			
	PRI	PAN	PRD	Undecided
Age				
18–24	43	29	8	14
25–29	47	19	11	17
30–39	45	19	9	19
40–49	50	12	10	19
50 +	48	12	8	19
Gender				
Male	42	22	10	18
Female	50	16	8	18
Education				
Primary or less	56	11	8	17
Secondary	42	22	10	17
College preparatory	35	25	13	22
University +	32	36	8	16
Income level				
A/B (highest levels)	37	35	6	14
C	33	33	9	17
D	46	18	8	19
E (lowest)	52	16	10	19
Size of locality				
Under 2,500 inhabitants	55	9	10	13
2,500–99,999	51	19	10	19
100,000–1 million	39	25	7	20
Over 1 million	38	24	9	13

Source: Belden & Russonello y Ciencia Aplicada, "México 1994: Resumen de una encuesta sobre preferencias electorales en México," *Este País* 44 (November 1994), special supplement, table 2. This table reports results from a nationwide preelection (July 23–August 1, 1994) sample survey of 1,526 probable voters, with an estimated sampling error of ±2.5 percentage points. The question regarding party preference was: "If the election were held today, for whom would you vote?" The responses were self-recorded, in private, on a sample ballot deposited secretly in a box carried by the interviewer.

"send a message" to the PRI-government apparatus (never intending to actually install an opposition government in power at the federal level), and to vote against the incumbent party at the state or local level, even if it is the PAN or the PRD.[20]

[20]Much recent survey data reflects this increasing volatility in Mexican voting behavior. See the analyses in Charles L. Davis and Kenneth M. Coleman, "Neoliberal Economic Policies and the Potential for Electoral Change in Mexico," *Mexican Studies* 10:2 (Summer 1994), pp. 341–70; Klesner, "The 1994 Mexican Elections"; and Jorge I. Domínguez and James A. McCann, "Shaping Mexico's Electoral Arena: The Construction of Partisan Cleavages in the 1988 and 1991 National Elections," *American Political Science Review* 89:1 (March 1995), pp. 34–48.

In the last three national elections, the PRI has done better among women than men (see, for example, table 4). This effect might be explained partly by the prevalence of women among the participants in grassroots organizations and committees that are affiliated with the PRI and, since 1989, with the government's National Solidarity Program.[21] Women may also be particularly susceptible to the PRI's incessant efforts to equate political change (especially in the form of an opposition party takeover of the government at the national level) with social disorder, violence, and economic chaos. Surveys show that the PRI's well-orchestrated "campaign of fear" was very effective in 1994—a year when violent events like the Chiapas rebellion and Luis Donaldo Colosio's assassination enlarged the so-called *voto de refugio* (people seeking refuge).[22]

In addition to rural voters and women, the PRI's core constituency also consists, increasingly, of older voters (though it did well among younger voters, as well, in 1994), the less educated, and low-income people.[23] It has also held the loyalty of most labor union members. However, many members of government-affiliated (CTM) unions feel compelled to vote for the PRI because of reprisals threatened by their local union bosses.[24] And the votes of Mexicans belonging to organizations affiliated with the PRI's other two sectors seem increasingly less influenced by the leadership of these corporatist structures.[25]

THE OPPOSITION PARTIES

Until recently, the opposition parties essentially performed a stabilizing, system-maintenance function in the Mexican political system. They gave the incumbent regime a loyal opposition in the Congress; provided an outlet for the protest vote (people so dissatisfied with the government's performance that they could not

[21]See Alejandra Massolo, *Por amor y coraje: mujeres en movimientos urbanos de la ciudad de México* (México, D.F.: El Colegio de México, 1992); and Nikki Craske, "Women and Regime Politics in Guadalajara's Low-Income Neighbourhoods," *Bulletin of Latin American Research* 13:1 (1994), pp. 61–78. Women were first allowed to vote in Mexico in 1958.

[22]Only 24 percent of the respondents in one national preelection survey believed that there was no possibility of violence following the 1994 elections; more than two-thirds feared either generalized or localized violence, regardless of who won the elections. (See Belden & Russonello y Ciencia Aplicada, "Resumen de una encuesta sobre preferencias electorales en México," figure 11.)

[23]See, for example, Tonatiuh Guillén López, "Political Parties and Political Attitudes in Chihuahua," in Arturo Alvarado, ed., *Electoral Patterns and Perspectives in Mexico* (La Jolla: Center for U.S.-Mexican Studies, University of California, San Diego, 1987), pp. 225–45.

[24]See Domínguez and McCann, "Shaping Mexico's Electoral Arena," table 2, p. 38.

[25]See, for example, Guadalupe Pacheco Méndez, "Estructura y resultados electorales," *Examen* (Consejo Ejecutivo Nacional, PRI) 2:15 (August 15, 1990), p. 20.

bring themselves to vote for PRI candidates, and who voted for whichever opposition party seemed strongest); and served as personal career vehicles for dissident political leaders, keeping them within the government-sanctioned arena of political competition. Internally fragmented and organizationally weak, the opposition parties could not attract sufficient electoral support to challenge PRI hegemony at the state or national levels. Leaders of these parties accepted seats in the Congress, occasionally criticized the government's policy decisions, and routinely negotiated election results with the PRI-government apparatus. The opposition parties' most basic function was to give the PRI something to run against, thereby strengthening the government's claim to popular support and legitimate authority.

The regime's basic strategy for dealing with the opposition parties was to "carry a big stick, and offer small carrots."[26] The carrots took the form of periodic tinkering with the federal election laws, so as to guarantee some level of representation for opposition parties in the Congress, make it easier for them to qualify for legal registration, and provide modest amounts of public financing for their campaigns.[27] By tolerating opposition parties and encouraging the formation of additional ones, especially to the left of the official party, the regime was able to channel most of the public discontent with its policies and performance through the electoral process, rather than risking violent antisystem protests.

In the late 1970s, and especially since 1985, a less pliant electoral opposition has emerged. Benefiting from the antigovernment sentiment provoked by the economic crisis and government austerity policies of the 1980s, opposition parties of the right and left became more formidable competitors. The PAN, in particular, sought support cutting across all social classes, hired full-time staff, and started conducting campaigns to win rather than simply to educate the citizenry. Opposition parties of both right and left became more willing to adopt civil disobedience and other confrontational tactics in their dealings with the government, especially to protest electoral fraud. Their representatives in the Congress challenged key national policies, such as the nationalization of the banking system in 1982, the continued servicing of Mexico's huge external debt, and accelerated economic integration with the United States via NAFTA. In these ways they have disputed the government's legitimacy, embarrassed it abroad, and raised the cost of political control and co-optation.

---

[26]Juan Molinar Horcasitas, *El tiempo de la legitimidad: elecciones, autoritarismo y democracia en México* (México, D.F.: Cal y Arena, 1991), p. 63.

[27]See Craig and Cornelius, "Houses Divided," pp. 290–97 ("Appendix: Major Changes in the Electoral Laws of Mexico").

In the national elections of August 1994, both of the main opposition parties made impressive gains, with the conservative PAN increasing its vote share by nearly 10 percentage points over 1988, and the left-of-center Partido de la Revolución Democrática (PRD) improving its performance by about 8 percentage points since the 1991 midterm elections. Nevertheless, with the opposition vote split eight ways (with the PAN, the PRD, and six other minor parties competing), the PRI's presidential candidate was able to prevail, even though more than half of the electorate voted for a change in government at the national level.

One of the electoral law "reforms" enacted under Salinas made it extremely difficult, if not practically impossible, for opposition parties to run fusion candidates for president (as five minor parties were able to do in 1988, by forming the Cardenista coalition). Therefore, a serious challenge to the PRI's continued control of the presidency is likely to result only from (1) an open rupture of the PRI, severely weakening its mobilizational and organizational capacity; and/or (2) an upsurge in support for one of the principal opposition parties, causing free-floating protest voters to coalesce around a single alternative to the PRI. However, the fragmentation of the *national-level* opposition vote does not prevent the election of more state governors, municipal presidents, and members of Congress from the opposition parties. For example, given foreseeable economic conditions and the Mexican voter's increasing disposition to punish the PRI-government apparatus for the economic mismanagement that led to crisis and hardship, the PRI could lose its majority in the federal Chamber of Deputies in the 1997 midterm elections.

Among Mexico's current opposition parties, the PAN is by far the best equipped to become a truly national party capable of challenging PRI dominance at all levels. Established in 1939, the PAN was formed largely in reaction to the leftward drift of public policy under President Lázaro Cárdenas. Its founders included prominent Catholic intellectuals who espoused a Christian Democratic ideology, and the party has traditionally opposed government restrictions on church activities. It attacked political centralism and advocated expanded states' rights, long before it was politically fashionable to do so.

The PAN has worked diligently to develop a strong network of grassroots militants capable of closely monitoring the electoral process and defending the party's vote. The PAN's regional strongholds include several northern border states (Baja California, Chihuahua, Sonora, and Nuevo León), the center-west states of Jalisco and Guanajuato, the Mexico City metropolitan area (Estado de México and the Federal District), and the southeastern state of

PAN presidential candidate Diego Fernández de Cevallos greets supporters at a campaign rally in the run-up to the 1994 election. Source: *Patricia Aridjis, by permission of Secretaría de Gobernación, Mexico.*

Yucatán. In these places, the PAN has managed to create a de facto two-party system, in which the PRI is clearly vulnerable to defeat. The margins of victory for the PAN's gubernatorial triumphs in the states of Baja California (in 1989) and Jalisco (in 1995) were so large that postelection protests by local PRI leaders were effectively preempted. In 1995, the PAN retained control of the governorship in Baja California, thereby accomplishing something that no opposition party had previously achieved: the transfer of power from one elected opposition governor to another.

President Zedillo found it expedient to appoint a prominent PAN leader, Antonio Lozano, to the most politically sensitive post in his cabinet, that of attorney general, and to make him responsible for implementing the new administration's top-priority political project: cleaning up the nation's police and judicial system and establishing the rule of law in all aspects of public life. Thus Lozano, who previously headed the PAN delegation in the federal Chamber of Deputies, became the first member of an opposition party to receive a cabinet appointment in a PRI administration.

While clearly the leader among Mexico's opposition parties in terms of organizational strength and ideological coherence, the PAN is a party with several major weaknesses. Since the mid-1970s it has been divided into moderate-progressive and militant-conservative ("neo-PANista") factions, which have jockeyed for control of the party machinery and carried out purges of opposing faction members when they were in power. The moderate-progressive faction, which advocates strategic alliances with the government on various issues, has clearly been in control of the party since 1989. The PAN has relatively few leaders of national stature, and since the mid-1980s it has had difficulty defining a national project or set of economic policies that constitutes a clear alternative to the government's programs. Under Presidents de la Madrid, Salinas, and Zedillo, the PAN saw many of its banners stolen by the PRI-government apparatus: free market-oriented economic policies, privatization of state-owned enterprises, closer ties with the United States, improved church-state relations, and authentic federalism.

Since the early 1980s, and particularly in its stronghold regions like the North, the PAN has made considerable progress in broadening its sources of support beyond its core constituency of younger, better-educated, city-dwelling, middle-class voters. In the 1988 national elections, the PAN won only 17 percent of the votes in small and medium-sized cities and 7 percent of the rural votes; in 1994, it took 26 percent of the vote in small and medium-sized cities and raised its share of the rural vote to 15 percent.[28] However, the PAN still has not penetrated deeply into isolated rural areas and impoverished urban neighborhoods, accounting for its reputation as the "asphalt party" (a party whose support extends only to the end of paved roads or streets). In the 1994 elections, for example, the PAN had poll watchers stationed in only one-third or fewer of the polling places in the country's most rural municipalities.[29]

The constraints on development of the leftist opposition parties in Mexico are rather different and more severe. Before 1988, the left had spawned political parties like the Partido Popular Socialista (PPS), which for decades served as a home for moderate socialists and other left-of-center politicians willing to collaborate with the government and even to endorse the PRI's presidential candidates, in exchange for a seat in Congress. The more independent left—that is, those who did not collaborate openly with the ruling party—was traditionally represented by the Partido Comunista Mexicano (PCM). The Communists were allowed to compete legally in elections during the presidency of Lázaro Cárdenas, but their party was subsequently outlawed and did not regain its

---

[28]See Eric Magar Meurs, "Elecciones municipales en el norte de México, 1970–1993," Tesis de Licenciatura en Ciencia Política, Instituto Tecnológico Autónomo de México, México, D.F., 1994; and Pacheco Méndez, "El nuevo mapa electoral," pp. 14–15.

[29]Fox, "National Electoral Choices in Rural Mexico," p. 20.

legal registration until 1979, when its congressional candidates won 5 percent of the vote.

During most of the 1980s, even in the face of Mexico's gravest economic crisis since the 1910 revolution, and despite a series of party mergers intended to reduce the fractionalization of the leftist vote, the parties to the left of the PRI lost ground electorally. They were hampered by constant internal squabbling (motivated by personalistic rivalries as well as ideological cleavages), an inability to do effective grassroots organizing, and an identification with discredited, statist economic policies.

The key to the left's rejuvenation in 1988 was a split within the PRI leadership—the most serious since the early 1950s. In August 1986 a number of nationally prominent PRI figures, all members of the party's center-left wing, formed a dissident movement within the PRI known as the Corriente Democrática (CD). They were led by Porfirio Muñoz Ledo (former head of the PRI, runner-up candidate for the party's presidential nomination in 1976, former secretary of labor and secretary of education), and Cuauhtémoc Cárdenas, who was just finishing his term as governor of the state of Michoacán. The CD criticized the de la Madrid administration's economic restructuring program and sought a renewed commitment by the PRI to traditional principles of economic nationalism and social justice. Most urgently, CD adherents called for a top-to-bottom democratization of the PRI, beginning with the elimination of the *dedazo* (unilateral selection by the outgoing president) as the mechanism for determining the party's presidential candidate. The CD's proposals were widely interpreted as a last-ditch attempt by the PRI's traditional *políticos* to recover leadership of the party by influencing the outcome of the 1987–1988 presidential succession. The CD's demands for reform were resoundingly rejected by the PRI hierarchy, and its leaders formally split from the party in October 1987.

Confronted with defeat within the PRI, Cárdenas accepted the presidential nomination of the Partido Auténtico de la Revolución Mexicana (PARM), a conservative, nationalist party established by another group of dissident PRIistas in 1954. Later, four other parties—all to the left of the PRI and including the remnants of the old Mexican Communist Party—joined the PARM to form a coalition, the Frente Democrático Nacional (FDN), to contest the 1988 presidential election, with Cárdenas as their candidate. Before joining the Cardenista coalition, the leftist parties had been attracting only insignificant support in public opinion polls, and some were in danger of losing their legal registration. As members of a center-left coalition led by a political figure with broad popular appeal, they stood to gain a great deal. Soon after the 1988 elections, however, the left's long-standing ideological and person-alistic cleavages reasserted themselves, and by 1991, when mid-term elections were held, most of Cárdenas's 1988 coalition part-ners had gone their separate ways, leaving the newly constituted PRD as the principal standard-bearer of the left. Even within the PRD, serious disagreements emerged over such issues as the degree of democracy in internal party governance and strategies for dealing with the government (dialogue and collaboration on certain issues versus permanent confrontation).

The PRD continues to take policy positions to the left of the ruling party on some issues (for example, arguing for a mor-atorium on external debt service, and insisting on renegotiation of some provisions of NAFTA); but the PRD has had difficulty developing a credible, alternative program of governance. Its differences with most recent government policies are matters of degree, pacing, and how much is being done to ameliorate the social costs of these policies, rather than their basic direction.

To an even greater extent than the PAN, the PRD is still a regional party, with strength concentrated in the states of Michoa-cán (Cárdenas's home base), the impoverished southern states (Guerrero, Oaxaca, Chiapas), and the Mexico City metropolitan area. The PRD has retained many of the urban, working-class voters who traditionally supported the parties of the independent left, but it has not been very successful in establishing ties with the new popular movements that have developed outside of the PRI-affiliated corporatist structures.

Today, Cuauhtémoc Cárdenas and other members of the more militant, intransigent wing of the PRD are often criticized for squandering a golden opportunity, created by the Cardenista coalition's strong showing in the 1988 elections, to consolidate the left as Mexico's second-most important political force. The PRD's congressional candidates collectively polled only 16.7 percent in the 1994 elections, and Cárdenas ran a poor third in his second presidential bid. Analyses of returns from federal and state elec-tions since 1989 show that the Cardenistas did a poor job of mobilizing previously uncommitted voters and self-described in-dependents.[30] This finding highlights the most serious deficiency of the Mexican left today: the lack of a strong, local-level infrastruc-ture—one that is not dependent on the personal charisma of Cuauhtémoc Cárdenas to mobilize PRD supporters, is capable of

---

[30]Domínguez and McCann, "Shaping Mexico's Electoral Arena," pp. 43–44; and Kathleen Bruhn and Keith Yanner, "Governing under the Enemy: The PRD in Michoacán," in Rodríguez and Ward, eds., *Opposition Government in Mexico*, pp. 115–19.

Cuauhtémoc Cárdenas, 1994 presidential candidate of the PRD, releases a dove at a campaign rally. To the left stands PRD party president Porfirio Muñoz Ledo. Source: *Víctor Mendiola; by permission of Secretaría de Gobernación, Mexico.*

defending the PRD vote against PRI fraud and intimidation, and can build a track record of successful governance.

From its inception, the PRD has been dominated by Mexico City–based politicians and intellectuals for whom the provinces hardly exist. Central PRD leaders have shortchanged local organizers in their allocation of the party's funds, on the grounds that scarce resources could be used most effectively to topple the PRI at the national level.[31] "The PRD has such weak links with its own base that the [national party] leadership decided to choose its 1994 Congressional candidates through backroom negotiations rather than open party primary elections."[32] The result is a party that is not equipped to win at the local and state levels, where, as the PAN has proven, Mexico's opposition parties have their greatest opportunities today.

But the left's problems in recent years have not all been self-inflicted. Under President Salinas, the government showed no inclination to negotiate seriously with the Cardenista left. Salinas's own contemptuous attitude toward the PRD was summed up in his public comment in response to protests by PRD legislators that

---

[31]See Kathleen M. Bruhn, *Taking on Goliath: The Emergence of a New Left Party and the Struggle for Democracy in Mexico* (University Park: Pennsylvania State University Press, forthcoming 1996).

[32]Jonathan Fox and Luis Hernández, "Lessons from the Mexican Elections," *Dissent* (Winter 1995), p. 32.

disrupted his final state of the nation address in November 1994: "I neither see them nor hear them." Under Salinas, the government showed much greater willingness to recognize electoral victories of the PAN than those claimed by the PRD, except for local offices in Cárdenas's home state of Michoacán. Conflicts between PRD militants and PRI *caciques* have been bitter, with more than 368 PRD activists murdered since the party was created in 1989. The behavior of the PRI-government apparatus in several key elections held during the Salinas *sexenio* signaled that it would never allow a PRD government to come to power at the state level, anywhere in the country. As noted above, President Zedillo has opened a new chapter in PRD-government relations, seeking to incorporate into his support base at least the moderate-pragmatic wing of the PRD, whose members are disposed to negotiating with the government.

Perhaps the greatest single obstacle to the institutionalization of a two-party or multiparty system in Mexico, with a realistic possibility of alternation in power at the national level, has been the PRI's ability to cast doubt on any opposition party's capacity to govern the country. In the 1988, 1991, and 1994 national elections, the PRI's fear-mongering—stressing that economic conditions would deteriorate and violence would erupt if some other party were to gain power—clearly resonated with a large segment of the electorate. For example, in a national preelection poll conducted in 1991, fully 87 percent of the respondents who believed that the national economy would suffer under an opposition party voted for the PRI.[33] Today, with the PRI's stewardship of the national economy and its ability to contain political violence now doubted by a large proportion of the electorate, opposition parties may have an unprecedented opportunity to overcome one of the PRI's last remaining advantages: fear of the unknown, which could hardly be worse than the reality the average Mexican now confronts.

---

[33]Domínguez and McCann, "Shaping Mexico's Electoral Arena," p. 41.

Campesinos, Organized Labor, and the Military: Pillars of the Regime?

The Mexican state's relationships with three major sectors of society—campesinos (peasants), organized labor, and the military—have been central to the stability of the regime since the 1930s. Indeed, these sectors are often referred to as pillars of the regime, in recognition of their crucial role in system maintenance. In recent years, however, the relationship or "pact" between Mexico's ruling elite and each of these three key sectors has been under extraordinary stress, and their continued support for the regime can no longer be taken for granted.

STATE-CAMPESINO RELATIONS

From 1810 until 1929 the Mexican peasantry was among the most rebellious in Latin America, engaging in frequent armed uprisings against both local and national elites.[1] After 1930, however, the rural poor became the largest support group of the Mexican government and of the official party. As a rule, this was the one segment of society that could always be counted on to vote for PRI candidates and to participate in electoral rallies and other regime-supportive activities. Perhaps more than any other segment of society, the low-income rural population believed in the ideals of the Mexican Revolution and in the government's intention to realize those ideals.

The campesino sector includes three important subgroups: landless wage laborers (*jornaleros*), beneficiaries of land reform (*ejidatarios*), and owners of very small properties (*minifundistas*). Their support was secured by two principal means: government policies that distributed vital resources (land, water, credit, fertil-

---

[1] See Friedrich Katz, ed., *Riot, Rebellion, and Revolution: Rural Social Conflict in Mexico* (Princeton, N.J.: Princeton University Press, 1988).

izer, and so on) to the rural population, and *caciquismo*—the most prevalent mode of political control in the countryside.

Traditionally, land has been the most important resource sought by campesinos, and land reform the most consistent government promise to them. Lázaro Cárdenas distributed more land, more rapidly, than any president before or since. Moreover, by establishing a nationwide confederation of campesino organizations, the Confederación Nacional Campesina (CNC), and incorporating it into the official party in 1938, Cárdenas institutionalized the relationship between the state and those campesinos who received land through the agrarian reform program. Other sectors of the campesino population—landless wage laborers and private landholders with very small plots—were not included in the CNC and have been marginalized in the distribution of government benefits to the rural sector.

The CNC's organizational dominance in the countryside has been contested increasingly by dissident groups. Four types of grievances have fueled independent campesino organizations: (1) unmet demands for land, especially in regions where large, undivided landholdings in excess of the legal size limit persist despite the existence of groups petitioning for land redistribution (the state of Chiapas has been the site of some of the most egregious cases); (2) complaints about low crop prices, set by the government; (3) limited access to markets (not a problem for large-scale agricultural producers); and (4) inequitable distribution of agricultural inputs like water and credit by government agencies and commercial banks (often biased in favor of larger producers). In addition, political grievances—usually rooted in the economic problems just mentioned—against *caciques* and corrupt municipal authorities have sometimes provoked campesino protests.

Despite the inroads made by autonomous movements since the late 1970s, most organized peasants in Mexico today are still members of CNC-affiliated organizations. However, the CNC's grip on the peasantry is increasingly tenuous, as demonstrated by the continuing erosion of the PRI's vote in rural areas. The CNC's dilemma is partly of its own making. The CNC leadership has become increasingly divorced from the confederation's social base. For many years, peasants have been manipulated, intimidated, and swindled by CNC leaders as well as by representatives of government agencies responsible for rural development programs.[2] Moreover, officials have often forged pernicious alliances with the *caciques* who control many *ejido* communities. These local

---

[2]For concrete examples, see Merilee S. Grindle, *Bureaucrats, Peasants, and Politicians in Mexico: A Case Study in Public Policy* (Berkeley: University of California Press, 1977), pp. 147–63.

bosses have amassed power and wealth by selling or renting *ejido* land to private farmers, with the acquiescence or active connivance of government officials.

Rural support for the regime has been undermined even more by major shifts in government policies since 1982 that have negatively affected campesino interests. The effects of these changes have been to bolster large-scale (especially export-oriented) agriculture, to make small-scale agriculture less viable, and to compel peasant farmers to make ends meet by selling much of their labor as migrant workers on large landholdings in Mexico or in the United States.[3]

Each of Mexico's last three presidents has publicly proclaimed the end of the government's land expropriation and redistribution program, begun in 1917, on the grounds that no more excessively large landholdings were available to be redistributed. The main function of the Agrarian Reform Ministry changed from processing peasants' petitions for land to granting certificates of "non-affectability" to cattle ranchers and other private landowners whose holdings exceed the legal limits, thereby protecting them from expropriation. The hunger for land persists: by the early 1990s, an estimated 32 percent of Mexico's rural population was landless.[4] Land hunger was a major underlying cause of the Zapatista rebellion in Chiapas, where 3,483 petitions for land—27 percent of the nation's total backlog—were unresolved as of 1992.[5]

Government policy in recent *sexenios* has emphasized the need to boost agricultural production by reorganizing the small *ejido* plots doled out through the agrarian reform program into larger, supposedly more efficient units of production—not to create additional small peasant producers. Indeed, the Salinas government hoped to sharply reduce the proportion of the nation's population employed in agriculture over the next ten years.[6] As an inducement to greater efficiency and recapitalization of land within the *ejido* sector, Article 27 of the constitution was amended in 1992 to permit

[3] Well-documented case studies of these effects can be found in Merilee S. Grindle, *Searching for Rural Development: Labor Migration and Employment in Mexico* (Ithaca, N.Y.: Cornell University Press, 1988); and Gail Mummert, *Tierra que pica* (Zamora, Mich.: El Colegio de Michoacán, 1994).

[4] Calculations from 1990 Population Census and 1991 Agricultural Census data by David Myhre. Compare Idriss Jazairy et al., *The State of World Rural Poverty* (New York: New York University Press, 1992), table 6, p. 407.

[5] Neil Harvey, with Luis Hernández Navarro and Jeffrey W. Rubin, *Rebellion in Chiapas: Rural Reforms, Campesino Radicalism, and the Limits to Salinismo*, 2d ed. (La Jolla: Center for U.S.-Mexican Studies, University of California, San Diego, 1994), p. 40.

[6] Former Undersecretary of Agriculture Luis Téllez, quoted in Wayne A. Cornelius, "The Politics and Economics of Reforming the Ejido Sector in Mexico," *Latin American Studies Association Forum* 23:3 (1992), p. 6.

(but not compel) the rental or sale of *ejido* plots to private farmers and groups of investors.[7] Early indications are that this historic change in rural land tenure rights will not cause a mass exodus of the current generation of mostly middle-aged or older *ejidatarios*. However, the next generation is much more disposed to sell the land they will inherit and emigrate.[8]

The efficacy of clientelistic PRI-government controls over the peasantry has also eroded as the resources available for supporting agriculture contracted, initially due to the economic crisis of the 1980s. Government price supports for most agricultural commodities have been slashed. The North American Free Trade Agreement and an overvalued peso were a boon to the large-scale agri-businessmen who could take advantage of them to increase production for export,[9] but these same policies have proven disastrous to small farmers. The latter can no longer afford to buy imported fertilizers, cattle fodder, seeds, and other inputs, while the prices they receive for fresh milk, meat, and other products have been depressed by a flood of processed-food imports from the United States and Canada. A sharp drop in agricultural credit available from government sources (beginning in 1989) and skyrocketing interest rates on loans from commercial banks (since 1994) now threaten to drive hundreds of thousands of small farmers into bankruptcy and off the land. As a result, "access to appropriate forms and adequate amounts of agricultural credit has become a key point of contention between campesino organizations and the Mexican state."[10]

The era of massive government subsidy and credit programs aimed at small-scale peasant agriculture—programs initiated in the early 1970s and vastly expanded during the oil boom years of 1980–1982—has ended. Social welfare programs like Solidarity and PROCAMPO fall far short of what is needed to maintain rural incomes and employment, much less to pay for irrigation, machinery, and other improvements. Without those improvements in

---

[7]See Cornelius, "The Politics and Economics of Reforming the Ejido Sector"; and Billie R. DeWalt, Martha N. Rees, and Arthur D. Murphy, *The End of Agrarian Reform in Mexico* (La Jolla: Center for U.S.-Mexican Studies, University of California, San Diego, 1994).

[8]Wayne A. Cornelius and David Myhre, eds., *The Transformation of Rural Mexico: Reforming the Ejido Sector* (La Jolla: Center for U.S.-Mexican Studies, University of California, San Diego, forthcoming 1996).

[9]See, for example, Judith Adler Hellman, *Mexican Lives* (New York: The New Press, 1994), pp. 139–51.

[10]David Myhre, "The Politics of Globalization in Rural Mexico: Campesino Initiatives to Restructure the Agricultural Credit System," in Philip McMichael, ed., *The Global Restructuring of Agro-Food Systems* (Ithaca, N.Y.: Cornell University Press, 1994), p. 147.

production technology, Mexico's small farmers will be unable to compete in liberalized commodity markets of global dimensions.

Thus, despite its need to retain a "safe" rural electoral base, it is not at all clear what benefits a technocratic government committed to fiscal discipline and letting market forces work will be able to offer to the small farmer—much less to Mexico's large population of landless rural workers—in the foreseeable future. Yet the opposition parties face formidable obstacles in penetrating the rural sector, where many people's livelihoods and voting behavior are still affected by local-level agents of the PRI-government apparatus.

THE STATE AND ORGANIZED LABOR

Since 1940, the Mexican government's control over organized labor has been essential to the strategy of economic development that the state has pursued. By tightly regulating the formation of new unions, wage increases, strike activity, and even the resolution of individual worker grievances against employers, the government has been able to guarantee a disciplined and relatively cheap labor force, attractive to both foreign and domestic investors. Government control over labor strikes has been especially tight and has grown progressively tighter over time. During the 1938–1945 period, an average of 32 percent of all workers' petitions for strikes were authorized (recognized as legal strikes) by the federal government; only 2 percent of all strike petitions were approved during the 1963–1988 period. Between 1982 and 1988, despite skyrocketing inflation and severe unemployment and underemployment problems, the level of authorized strike activity actually declined.[11] As they have done during the economic crisis of the mid-1990s, most labor leaders took the position that protecting jobs and restoring national economic stability must be the top priorities. This means cooperating with management by, for example, making contract concessions and urging union members to boost productivity—not threatening work stoppages.

Minimum wage levels set by the federal government traditionally have determined the negotiating framework for plant-level union officials throughout the country. Beginning in 1983, the PRI-affiliated CTM—which claims 5 million members—served as an active and essential partner in the government's economic stabilization efforts, usually settling for wage increases far below the rate of inflation. From 1987 to 1995, the CTM leadership signed a series

---

[11]See Kevin J. Middlebrook, *The Paradox of Revolution: Labor, the State, and Authoritarianism in Mexico* (Baltimore, Md.: Johns Hopkins University Press, 1995), table 5.1, p. 165.

of economic solidarity pacts with the government and the business community—an arrangement that kept wages under tight control even while allowing many prices to rise.

Unlike virtually all other labor federations in Latin America during the last ten years, the CTM has not opposed the government's policy of privatizing state-owned enterprises (often resulting in significant job losses) nor other policies intended to restructure the country's economy along free-market lines. Also in contrast to most other Latin American labor movements, organized labor in Mexico has joined the government in resisting "excessively" rapid political liberalization. Indeed, while professing to be the staunchest guardian of Mexico's revolutionary heritage, organized labor has become the most conservative sector of the ruling coalition. The CTM hierarchy has advocated hard-line responses to most forms of political dissent and has resisted any changes in the rules of electoral competition that would benefit opposition parties. After the Cardenistas defected from the PRI in 1987, Fidel Velázquez became the most vociferous opponent of government "concessions" to the Cardenista party (that is, recognition of its electoral victories). Velázquez and other *oficialista* labor leaders apparently feared that the reformist impulse might spread beyond the electoral system to the labor movement itself, strengthening pressures for greater democracy within CTM-affiliated unions, which have been run like political machines.

The government-affiliated unions have also helped to maintain political control by keeping lower-class demand making fragmented. From 1955 to about 1975, through a steady stream of government-orchestrated wage increases and expansions of nonwage benefits (subsidized food, clothing, housing, health care, transportation, and the like), the government created a privileged elite of unionized workers within the urban working class. These nonwage benefits served as a cushion during the economic crisis of the 1980s, partially insulating unionized workers from the ravages of high inflation and government austerity measures.

Of the three main sectors of the PRI, it has been the labor sector that has been the strongest and best organized for collective political action. Unionized workers could be mobilized quickly and on a national scale to participate in demonstrations to support controversial government policies, campaign rallies, voter registration drives, and the running of polling places. Organized labor's representatives—especially the members of the national teachers' union—have been very important to the PRI in mobilizing its vote in rural areas and small towns.

From the government's viewpoint, the high degree of continuity in CTM leadership has also been a vital asset. Fidel Velázquez has been the undisputed leader of the government-affiliated labor movement since 1949. Although several of the nine presidents under whom Velázquez has served have had sharp policy disagreements with him, there is no question that his long reign and political dexterity have contributed greatly to the stability of the Mexican political system. By the same reasoning, Velázquez's death (he was born in 1900) could release centrifugal forces within the labor movement that could complicate, at least temporarily, the government's relations with organized labor, since Velázquez's successor is unlikely to be as slavishly supportive of the regime and its antilabor macroeconomic policies as he has been.

Unable to secure significant concessions from the government on the wage front since the early 1980s, the CTM shifted its emphasis to safeguarding workers' purchasing power through the creation of union-owned retail stores, consumer cooperatives, and other "social sector" enterprises. The CTM also sought and received (until 1991) modest increases in political patronage. For example, the share of congressional seats allocated by the PRI leadership to the labor sector rose from 14 percent in 1976 to 22 percent in 1988. Although political patronage is of limited benefit to rank-and-file union members, it helped to maintain the support of the CTM leadership for government policies.

Independent unionism gained a small foothold in the labor movement during the 1970s, mainly among university faculty and staff employees, and workers in the automobile, mining, electrical, telephone, and nuclear energy industries. Technological changes and deteriorating working conditions in these industries had created new worker grievances that were being ignored by established union organizations.[12] In 1979 a dissident movement emerged within the national teachers' union, and by 1989 it had gained enough support to stage a nationwide strike by half a million teachers. This gave President Carlos Salinas sufficient pretext to force the resignation of the union's long-entrenched president, Carlos Jonguitud Barrios.[13]

Despite sporadic triumphs, independent unionism and its causes have not progressed very far in Mexico. Widely detested union *caciques* like Jonguitud and Joaquín Hernández Galicia ("La Quina"), the head of the oil workers' union, also deposed by Salinas in 1989, were replaced by leaders handpicked by the president, not democratically elected by union members. In many industries and regions, heavy-handed, authoritarian control of unionized workers by labor union bosses persists.

---

[12]For an example from the Mexican automobile industry, see Middlebrook, *The Paradox of Revolution*, pp. 228–36.

[13]For a case study of the origins and development of dissidence within the teachers' union, see Foweraker, *Popular Mobilization in Mexico*.

Independent unions have not won the ability to organize national-level unions that could compete against the large, nationally organized, CTM-affiliated unions for the support of workers. Thus, the most militant independent union movements remain localized and isolated. The government provides economic subsidies and political protection to its allies within the labor movement, while using its regulatory controls over union registration and strike activity to discipline potential opponents and create divisions within dissident movements.

The economic crisis that erupted in December 1994 was of such severity that it provoked leaders of several major labor unions that are not part of the CTM to take an increasingly assertive and critical stance toward the government's economic and social policies. The head of the teachers' union, for example, complained that Mexico had, apparently, chosen to become a "cheap-labor economy with little in the way of a social safety net and where productivity rose only because people were made to work harder for less."[14] In truth, however, neither more independent-minded unions nor the *oficialista* labor movement have much leverage with the government and private employers in the present environment of economic uncertainty and rising international competition. The restructuring of Mexico's economy since the early 1980s has worked to labor's disadvantage in various ways. For example, employment in the most easily organizable sectors—heavy industry and the public sector, including state-owned firms—has fallen, while job growth has become concentrated in regions and sectors of the economy (for instance, the *maquiladora* light manufacturing industry in northern border cities) that are less hospitable to union organizing.[15] Moreover, the economic crisis of the 1990s is likely to shrink employment in the formal sector, while Mexicans displaced from formal-sector jobs or those newly entering the work force will be seeking employment in the unorganized, informal sector. This means that the unionized portion of Mexico's work force—probably no more than 10 to 12 percent of the total economically active population in the mid-1990s—is likely to decline significantly in the years to come.[16]

---

[14]Esther Gordillo, quoted in *Mexico and NAFTA Report* (London), RM-95-11, November 2, 1995, p. 7.

[15]See Leslie Sklair, *Assembling for Development: The Maquila Industry in Mexico and the United States*, 2d ed. (La Jolla: Center for U.S.-Mexican Studies, University of California, San Diego, 1993), pp. 104–05; and Middlebrook, *The Paradox of Revolution*, pp. 320–21.

[16]Precise figures on union members as a proportion of the economically active population are not available. The most recent, reliable statistics were generated in 1978, well before the economic crises of the 1980s and mid-1990s. See Middlebrook, *The Paradox of Revolution*, fn. 65, p. 420.

In all probability, however, *oficialista* labor leaders will continue to deliver a significant portion of the PRI's vote, because this is their best insurance policy against union democratization and against the erosion of their remaining pockets of power within the PRI-government apparatus. At the same time, their bargaining power vis-à-vis the state—like that of the Mexican labor movement as a whole—will continue to erode, as more working-class Mexicans desert the PRI for opposition parties.

THE MILITARY IN POLITICS

By the end of the Cárdenas era, Mexico had a largely demilitarized political system: Political activity by high-ranking military men had been confined to nonviolent competition and bargaining, within an institutionalized decision-making framework that was clearly dominated by civilian elites. Beginning with Calles in the 1920s, Mexican presidents used three basic tools to achieve military disengagement from politics: frequent rotation of military zone commanders (to prevent them from building up large personal followings of troops and local politicians); generous material incentives for staying out of politics; and a policy of requiring military men who wanted to remain politically active to do so essentially as private individuals rather than as representatives of the military as an institution.

The number of military men serving in nonmilitary public offices has declined steadily, from 27 percent during the second half of the Cárdenas administration (1935–1940) to 5 percent in the de la Madrid *sexenio* (1982–1988).[17] Up to 1964 it was traditional for the president to appoint a military officer to serve in the post of PRI chairman; since then, that position has been held only by career politicians. Typically, the only cabinet posts now held by active military officers are secretary of national defense and secretary of the navy. State governorships held by career military officers dropped from 48 percent under Lázaro Cárdenas to 3 to 5 percent during the Díaz Ordaz, Echeverría, López Portillo, and de la Madrid *sexenios*, to none under Salinas.[18] During the 1988–1991 congressional term, military officers (on leave from active duty) held just 3 of the 64 Senate seats and 4 of the 500 seats in the Chamber of Deputies.

The most striking indicator of the military's decline as a political institution is its share of total government expenditures, which dropped from 17 percent in 1940, to 5 to 6 percent in the 1970s, to

---

[17]Roderic A. Camp, *Generals in the Palacio: The Military in Modern Mexico* (New York: Oxford University Press, 1992), table 4-1, p. 67.

[18]Ibid., table 4-2, p. 69.

about 2 percent in the 1980s. As a percentage of gross domestic product, Mexico's military expenditures averaged less than 1 percent during the 1960–1984 period—the lowest of any Latin American country, including Costa Rica, which has only a national police force. Spending on the military has increased moderately in recent years, partly in response to U.S. pressure on the Mexican government to step up its drug eradication and interdiction efforts. By 1995 Mexico had about 150,000 men under arms, over one-quarter of whom were supposed to be engaged full time in the antidrug campaign. The military's generally positive image among the Mexican public has been cemented over the years by its *labor social*: high-visibility visits to rural communities and urban slums to provide services ranging from free medical and dental treatment to haircuts, tree planting, and refurbishing of schoolrooms.

By the standards of most Latin American countries, the Mexican military is impoverished in terms of hardware, but successive governments have taken care to provide a steady flow of material benefits for military personnel. They have received regular salary increases (even during the worst years of economic crisis and government austerity budgets) and a variety of generous nonwage benefits (housing, medical care, loans, subsidized consumer goods) which added about 40 percent to base pay.

Despite the long-term decline in its influence on government policy making, the Mexican military retains a capacity to affect political events that may have wide ramifications. Civilian presidents still call on the military for support during political and economic crises. In recent *sexenios* such support has taken the form of armed repression of dissident groups (as in the 1968 massacre of student demonstrators in Mexico City, and the 1990 ejection of Cardenista militants from 16 town halls in Michoacán which they had occupied to protest electoral fraud); counterinsurgency campaigns against rural guerrillas in the 1960s, 1970s, and the mid-1990s; the breaking of major, unauthorized labor stoppages, such as a strike at Cananea, the country's largest mine, in 1989; the arrest of powerful political figures accused of committing criminal offenses (for example, "La Quina," head of the oil workers' union); and the promulgation of a harsh, new economic stabilization plan in 1995. In all of these cases, "the military did not ask to be involved but was brought into the decision-making process when trouble was at hand."[19] Similarly, as the Echeverría and López Portillo *sexenios* were drawing to a close, amid fiscal chaos and erratic presidential behavior, rumors spread that the military would seize control of the government. In both cases, top-ranking military

---

[19]Ibid., p. 223.

officers helped to bring an end to the rumor campaign and to guarantee a nonviolent transfer of power to a new civilian president simply by publicly reaffirming their loyalty to the nation's institutional order.

Since the mid-1980s, civilian authorities confronted with a more aggressive electoral opposition have expanded the military's political control functions—much to the distaste of some officers. They have called on the military to provide highly visible "security" before, during, and sometimes after hotly contested elections. Opposition parties have charged that the huge military presence in such cases was intended to intimidate their supporters, reducing the likelihood that they would go to the polls and take to the streets to protest vote fraud if it occurred. The routinized use of the military for political control could strain civil-military relations. "The military doesn't like to perform police functions," complained one general.[20]

During the Salinas *sexenio*, civil-military relations were strained by mounting evidence that the military has been deeply penetrated by drug traffickers seeking protection. President Salinas's first secretary of the navy was publicly implicated in a drug-protection scandal but was allowed to resign without being prosecuted. The rebellion in Chiapas created additional stresses. During the initial phase, the military was ordered by the Salinas administration to use lethal force to put down the insurrection. When President Salinas declined to defend the military against charges by the media and nongovernmental organizations of significant human rights violations committed during its operations in Chiapas, the secretary of national defense felt compelled to launch his own public relations campaign to defend the military institution. When President Zedillo briefly resumed armed hostilities against the Zapatista rebels in February 1995, after a one-year truce, his action was widely viewed as a concession to the military, which had become fed up with governmental inaction in Chiapas.

Clearly, civil-military relations in Mexico have entered a new era of uncertainty and occasionally acute strain.[21] But precisely because the military remains one of few enduring pillars of support for the PRI-government apparatus, at a time when the potential for social protest is high, it is probable that Zedillo will follow

---

[20]General Luis Garfías, remarks at the "Research Workshop on the Modern Mexican Military," Center for U.S.-Mexican Studies, University of California, San Diego, March 1984.

[21]See Stephen J. Wager and Donald S. Schulz, *The Awakening: The Zapatista Revolt and Its Implications for Civil-Military Relations and the Future of Mexico* (Carlisle, Penn.: Strategic Studies Institute, 1994); and Wager, "Chiapas y las relaciones entre civiles y militares," *Este País* 49 (April 1995), pp. 12–17.

the example set by all of his predecessors since the 1940s. Each has reaffirmed a policy of honoring the military effusively in public rhetoric, respecting its autonomy in promotions and other matters of internal governance, maintaining the flow of material rewards to military personnel, and not allowing momentary clashes of will with the military hierarchy to get out of hand.[22]

Recent presidents have also supported a major upgrading of military education. By 1985 the military education system included a new National Defense College conferring a master's degree in national security and defense management, and 22 other schools that offered training in a wide range of professions and technical skills. This expansion of educational opportunities has "increased the military's capacity to take on new political functions should Mexico suddenly experience a crisis of governability, or if civil-military relations deteriorated beyond a certain point."[23]

Most observers, however, do not anticipate the reemergence of the military as an independent political actor, *unless* the country's civilian rulers fail completely to maintain law and order.[24] A very widespread, totally uncontrolled mass mobilization—whatever its origins—might well provoke a military intervention, more likely intended to restore order than to install a military government. It is the malfunctioning of civilian authority, rather than the military's own ambitions, that would be most likely to cause the military to assume an overt political role once again.

---

[22]See Stephen J. Wager, "The Mexican Army, 1940–1982: The Country Comes First," Ph.D. dissertation, Stanford University, 1992.

[23]José Luis Piñeyro, "The Modernization of the Mexican Armed Forces," in Augusto Varas, ed., *Democracy under Siege: New Military Power in Latin America* (Westport, Conn.: Greenwood Press, 1989), p. 116.

[24]See, for example, David Ronfeldt, ed., *The Modern Mexican Military: A Reassessment* (La Jolla: Center for U.S.-Mexican Studies, University of California, San Diego, 1984); and Camp, *Generals in the Palacio*, pp. 228–30.

Political Culture and Socialization

Most of what we know empirically about Mexican political culture is based on research completed during the period of sustained economic growth and virtually unchallenged one-party rule in Mexico, from 1940 to the mid-1970s. There is a growing body of survey-based research on attitudes toward political parties and other elements of mass political culture in the 1980s and 1990s, but not yet enough to confidently document the changes in core values, attitudes, and behaviors that most observers assume have occurred during the last two decades of economic and political crises.

The portrait of Mexican political culture that emerges from pre-1976 studies can be summarized as follows: Mexicans are highly supportive of the political institutions that evolved from the Mexican Revolution, and they endorse the democratic principles embodied in the constitution of 1917. However, they are critical of government performance, especially in creating jobs, reducing social and economic inequality, and delivering basic public services. Most government bureaucrats and politicians are viewed as distant, elitist, and self-serving, if not corrupt. Mexicans traditionally have been pessimistic about their ability to affect election outcomes, anticipating fraud and regarding voting and attendance at campaign rallies as ritualistic activities.[1]

On the surface, this combination of attitudes and beliefs seems to be internally contradictory. How could Mexicans support a political system that they see as unresponsive or capricious at best, in which they are mere "subjects" rather than true participants? Historically, popular support for the Mexican political system has

[1]For a critical review of the literature from which this portrait of Mexican political culture is assembled, see Ann L. Craig and Wayne A. Cornelius, "Political Culture in Mexico: Continuities and Revisionist Interpretations," in Gabriel Almond and Sidney Verba, eds., *The Civic Culture Revisited* (Newbury Park, Calif.: Sage Publications, 1989), pp. 325–93.

derived from three sources: the revolutionary origins of the regime, the government's role in promoting economic growth, and its performance in distributing concrete, material benefits to a substantial proportion of the Mexican population since the Cárdenas era. Each of these traditional sources of support has been undermined to some extent since 1982.

The official interpretation of the 1910 revolution stresses symbols (or myths) such as social justice, democracy, the need for national unity, and the popular origins of the current regime. The government's identification with these symbols has been constantly reinforced by the mass media, public schools, and the mass organizations affiliated with the official party. Over the years, the party's electoral appeals were explicitly designed to link its candidates with agrarian reform and other revered ideals of the revolution, with national heroes like Emiliano Zapata and Lázaro Cárdenas, and with the national flag. (The PRI emblem conveniently has the same colors, in the same arrangement.) Beginning in 1987, the neo-Cardenista opposition mounted the first serious challenge to the PRI and government's claim to the revolutionary mantle.

Relatively few Mexicans have based their support for the system primarily on its revolutionary origins or symbolic outputs, however. For most sectors of the population, symbols had to be supplemented with particularistic material rewards: plots of land or titles to land that had been occupied illegally, schools, low-cost medical care, agricultural crop price supports, government-subsidized food and other consumer goods, and public-sector jobs. For more than 40 years, the personal receipt of some material "favor" from the official party–government apparatus, or the hope that such benefits might be received in the future, ensured fairly high levels of mass support for the system.

Despite their keen dissatisfaction with the government's recent economic performance, electoral corruption, police abuses, environmental pollution, and many other irritations, the vast majority of Mexicans have remained "system loyalists." Survey data collected during the 1980s and early 1990s consistently revealed the Mexican people's fundamental aversion to concepts of radical transformation. A Gallup poll conducted in May 1988 showed that 61 percent of Mexicans thought that an opposition party victory at the national level would damage the country's economic prospects.[2] In a 1994 preelection survey, only 36 percent of a national sample of registered voters hoped that an opposition party would

[2]Dan Williams, "Polls Becoming an Issue in Mexico's Campaign," *Los Angeles Times*, June 28, 1988.

actually win, in order to bring about basic change in the country.[3] In short, at least prior to the economic collapse of the mid-1990s, the public opinion data reveal a citizenry still tethered to its traditional political moorings.

Nevertheless, most Mexicans today do not hesitate to criticize the way in which the system functions, and many more of them feel free to demonstrate their dissatisfaction with government performance by voting to throw the rascals out, especially in state and local elections, where the perceived risks of an opposition party takeover are lower. Surveys show that Mexicans at all income levels are concerned about "bad government." Their assessments of politics, politicians, government bureaucrats, and the police are predominantly cynical and mistrustful.[4] Corruption is assumed to be pervasive, but historically most Mexicans tolerated it, within limits, as a price to be paid in order to extract benefits from the system or to deal with police harassment.[5] The unbridled corruption of the López Portillo and Salinas *sexenios* drastically reduced such tolerance, however. Moreover, a recent upsurge in drug-related corruption, reaching into the highest levels of the government bureaucracy and the national security apparatus, has angered Mexicans and led many to fear that their government was being taken over by *"narco-políticos"* — public officials in league with corrupt police and drug lords.

During the last 20 years, Mexicans increasingly have blamed their personal economic distress on failures of government performance. In previous decades, the government received much credit for stimulating and guiding the nation's economic development. The deep economic recessions, inflationary spirals, and currency devaluations of the 1970s, 1980s, and 1990s have largely wiped out those positive perceptions. Particularly among middle-class Mexicans, many of whom saw their personal assets and living standards decline precipitously during this period, loss of confidence in the government's ability to manage the economy has been dramatic.

MASS POLITICAL SOCIALIZATION

How do Mexicans form their attitudes toward the political system? In addition to the family, the schools are an important source of preadult political learning. All schools, including church-affiliated

[3]Belden & Russonello y Ciencia Aplicada, "Resumen de una encuesta sobre preferencias electorales en México," figure 12, p. 8.

[4]See the national survey data reported in Alberto Hernández and Luis Navarro Rodríguez, eds., *Como somos los mexicanos* (México, D.F.: Centro de Estudios Educativos, 1987), p. 22.

[5]See Stephen D. Morris, *Corruption and Politics in Contemporary Mexico* (Tuscaloosa: University of Alabama Press, 1991).

and lay private schools, must follow a government-approved curriculum and use the same set of free textbooks, written by the federal Ministry of Education. Although the private schools' compliance with the official curriculum is often nominal, control over the content of textbooks gives the government an instrument for socializing children to a formal set of political values. This learning supports national political institutions and stresses the social and economic progress that has been made under postrevolutionary governments. Its impact is reflected in the beliefs of Mexican schoolchildren that their country has experienced a true social revolution; that, although this revolution is still incomplete, the government is working diligently to realize its goals; and that the president is an omnipotent authority figure, whose principal function is to "maintain order in the country."[6] Thus, despite the many egregious failures of presidential leadership that Mexicans have witnessed since the late 1960s, most of them continue to express a preference for strong, presidentialist government.

The Catholic Church is another source of values conditioning political attitudes among some Mexicans. Private, church-run schools have proliferated in recent years; and along with secular private schools, they provide education for a large portion of children from middle- and upper-class families. Religious schools and priests traditionally have preached against socialism, criticized anticlerical laws and policies, and promoted individual initiative (as opposed to governmental action). They also stress the need for moral Christian behavior, which is seen as absent in the corrupt, self-serving, materialistic world of politics. However, the direct influence of the church and religion in general on political behavior in Mexico may be weaker than commonly believed. For example, data from national surveys conducted in 1988 and 1991 reveal no difference in frequency of church attendance between PRI and PAN voters, despite the stereotype of PANistas as being ardently pro-clerical.[7]

Research on Mexican political culture shows that attitudes such as political efficacy (a sense of competence to influence the political process), cynicism about politicians, and evaluations of government performance in delivering goods and services are strongly influenced by political learning that occurs *after* childhood and adolescence.[8] As adults, Mexicans learn much about politics from their personal encounters with PRI and government

---

[6]Rafael Segovia, *La politización del niño mexicano* (México, D.F.: El Colegio de México, 1975), pp. 51–58.

[7]Domínguez and McCann, "Shaping Mexico's Electoral Arena," table 2, p. 38.

[8]For examples, see Wayne A. Cornelius, *Politics and the Migrant Poor in Mexico City* (Stanford, Calif.: Stanford University Press, 1975).

functionaries and, increasingly, by participating in local community-based organizations and popular movements that seek collective benefits or redress of grievances of various sorts from the government. There has been an impressive proliferation of popular movements in Mexico since 1968, when the student protest movement was launched and violently repressed.[9] The catalysts for this new wave of popular movements have included *oficialista* labor union gangsterism, increasingly blatant PRI vote fraud in state and local elections during the 1980s, the nationalization of Mexico's banks by President José López Portillo in 1982, the fumbling government response to the Mexico City earthquakes of 1985, the debate over NAFTA, and the implementation of a variety of domestic, neoliberal economic policies that adversely affected low- and middle-class segments of the society.

While most of these popular movements have been quite localized in scope and concerns, a few have grown to embrace thousands of Mexicans in many different states. Examples include the dissident teachers' union movement that began in the late 1970s[10] and the El Barzón movement, formed in 1993 to represent agricultural producers in the state of Jalisco who were past due on loan payments to private banks. After the 1994–1995 peso devaluation, El Barzón quickly mushroomed into a nationwide, mostly middle-class protest movement against soaring interests rates on all sorts of consumer and small-business credit. In the electoral arena, the Civic Alliance—a coalition of hundreds of nongovernmental organizations, independent labor unions, and popular movements—mobilized 18,280 Mexican citizens and 450 foreign visitors throughout the country to scrutinize the conduct of the August 21, 1994, elections.[11]

Have these and the hundreds of other, more modestly scaled popular movements that emerged in recent years actually changed Mexican political culture? The jury is still out on this question.[12] At

---

[9]See Foweraker and Craig, eds., *Popular Movements and Political Change in Mexico*; and Paul L. Haber, "The Art and Implications of Political Restructuring in Mexico: The Case of Urban Popular Movements," in Maria L. Cook, Kevin J. Middlebrook, and Juan Molinar Horcasitas, eds., *The Politics of Economic Restructuring: State-Society Relations and Regime Change in Mexico* (La Jolla: Center for U.S.-Mexican Studies, University of California, San Diego, 1994), pp. 277–303.

[10]See Foweraker, *Popular Mobilization in Mexico*.

[11]See Aguayo Quezada, "A Mexican Milestone"; and Michael C. Taylor, "Civic Alliance: The Emergence of a Political Movement in Contemporary Mexico," senior honors thesis in social studies, Harvard College, March 1995.

[12]For two contrasting views, see Diane E. Davis, "Failed Democratic Reform in Contemporary Mexico: From Social Movements to the State and Back Again," *Journal of Latin American Studies* 26:2 (May 1994), pp. 375–408; and Joe Foweraker, "Popular Movements and Political Culture in Contemporary Mexico," *Journal of Latin American Studies* 27 (1995).

Long lines of prospective voters formed early on August 21, 1994, to cast their ballots in Mexico's cleanest and highest-turnout presidential election to date. This line, at a polling place in Mexico City, stretched for an entire city block. An observer from Alianza Cívica, a nongovernmental organization that dispatched Mexican-citizen and foreign poll watchers to a national sample of 1,810 voting places, can be seen in the upper right corner. Source: *Yolanda Andrade; by permission of Secretaría de Gobernación, Mexico.*

minimum, the very accumulation of popular movements and their growing capacity to disrupt "normal" political and economic life has forced the government to pay more attention to developments in civil society occurring outside of the framework of state-sanctioned and manipulated organizations, and to increase its responsive capability in a variety of areas. As one Mexican social scientist has observed, "The important point is that the government in Mexico is losing its ability to make decisions in isolation from public opinion." Nor can it be argued any longer that Mexico's authoritarian political *institutions* are "sustained by an equally authoritarian political *culture* . . . characterized by passive submission to the dictates of authority and a citizenry that believes itself incapable of influencing the exercise of power."[13]

The 150,000 local committees established to implement the Salinas administration's National Solidarity Program were also intended, at least by the program's initial designers, to promote a new kind of political learning, by encouraging active citizen partic-

---

[13]Soledad Loaeza, "The Emergence and Legitimization of the Modern Right, 1970–1988," in Cornelius, Gentleman, and Smith, eds., *Mexico's Alternative Political Futures*, pp. 351, 353.

ipation in setting government resource allocation priorities, making local government more responsive, and increasing financial accountability. Again, any assessment of how much the Solidarity program has contributed to the emergence of a new, more participatory political culture in Mexico would be premature. However, early research suggests that the kind of socialization acquired through Solidarity Committees varies widely. A study done in three northern border cities found that only about a tenth of the population benefiting from Solidarity projects were personally engaged in these programs in a potentially "transformative" way — that is, participating in them in a way that transcends purely instrumental activity aimed at increasing one's capacity to extract material benefits from the political system, and that creates conditions necessary for fundamental change in the citizen-state relationship.[14]

In sum, Mexicans have been taught two sets of political values that increasingly seem to be in conflict.[15] On the one hand, mainly through the schools, they are formally taught a normative set of values about revolutionary institutions and objectives that identify the general public interest with the political system. On the other hand, adult experiences teach them how Mexican politics "really works." They are exposed to the corruption, patronage, intimidation, and violence practiced by petty PRI bosses, union officials, police, paid informers, thugs, and other agents of the regime.[16] The opposition parties (whose militants are frequently the targets of official violence) have sought to capitalize on the perceived gap between democratic-constitutional values and "real" politics.

As noted above, support for the PRI has been declining among the better-educated population. Education has increased criticism of the electoral system and reduced tolerance for human rights violations by the government and security forces. Higher levels of education are also associated with stronger support for the right to dissent and other democratic liberties.[17]

---

[14]See Oscar F. Contreras and Vivienne Bennett, "National Solidarity in the Northern Borderlands: Social Participation and Community Leadership," in Cornelius, Craig, and Fox, eds., *Transforming State-Society Relations in Mexico*, pp. 281–305.

[15]See Kenneth M. Coleman and Charles L. Davis, *Politics and Culture in Mexico* (Ann Arbor: Institute for Social Research, University of Michigan, 1988).

[16]For vivid portrayals of how these staples of Mexican political life have been experienced by 15 citizens of widely differing income levels, see Hellman, *Mexican Lives*.

[17]John Booth and Mitchell Seligson, "The Political Culture of Authoritarianism in Mexico: A Reexamination," *Latin American Research Review* 19 (1984), pp. 106–24; and Joseph L. Klesner, "Changing Patterns of Electoral Participation and Official Party Support in Mexico," in Judith Gentleman, ed., *Mexican Politics in Transition* (Boulder, Colo.: Westview, 1987), pp. 95–127.

POLITICAL PARTICIPATION

Traditionally, most political participation in Mexico has been of two broad types: (1) ritualistic, regime-supportive activities (for example, voting, attending campaign rallies), and (2) petitioning or contacting of public officials to influence the allocation of some public good or service. People participated in PRI campaign rallies mostly because attending might have a specific material payoff (a free meal, a raffle ticket, a tee-shirt), or because failure to do so could have personal economic costs. For example, union members who failed to attend such rallies could expect to lose a day's pay. As they went to the polls, Mexicans knew that they were not selecting those who would govern but merely ratifying the choice of candidates made earlier by the PRI-government hierarchy. Some voted because they regarded it as their civic duty; others because they wished to avoid difficulty in future dealings with government agencies. (By law, voting is obligatory in Mexico, and evidence of having voted in the most recent election has sometimes been required to receive public services.) Some voted in response to pressures from local *caciques* and PRI sector representatives. And some, especially in rural areas, sold their votes to get favors from local officials.[18]

As elections have become moments of genuine political confrontation in many parts of Mexico, however, the ritualistic quality of voting and participation in campaign activities has diminished. Mexico today is in the midst of an explosion in political participation, as evidenced not only by the virtually nonstop protests of citizens' movements of all types (in 1993 alone, 608 mass demonstrations were held in the Zócalo, Mexico City's historic central plaza[19]) but also by a dramatic rise in turnout in federal and state elections. The turnout of registered voters rose from 49 percent in the 1988 presidential election, to 61 percent in the midterm 1991 elections, to 78 percent in the 1994 presidential election—a 28 percentage-point increase in six years (see figure 3). Some 96 percent of Mexico's voting-age population was registered to vote in 1994.

Unfortunately, valid comparisons with electoral participation rates in the pre-1988 period are impossible, since the 1988 presidential election was the first for which reasonably accurate turnout figures were made public. In all previous national elections, the

---

[18]Such vote-selling behavior apparently persisted in the 1994 national elections. See Jonathan Fox, "Governance and Rural Development in Mexico: State Intervention and Public Accountability," *Journal of Development Studies* 32:1 (October 1995), pp. 19–20.

[19]Alejandra Massolo, "La politización de lo cotidiano," *Este País* 46 (January 1995), p. 4.

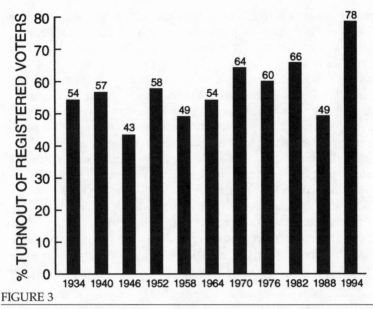

FIGURE 3

TURNOUT OF REGISTERED VOTERS IN PRESIDENTIAL ELECTIONS, 1934–1994*

Source: Data from Comisión Federal Electoral (for 1934–1988); from Instituto Federal Electoral (for 1994).

*The eligible electorate for 1934 through 1952 includes all males aged 21 or over. Women received the franchise in 1958. Beginning in 1970, the legal voting age was lowered to 18.

government inflated turnout statistics, in an effort to convince Mexicans and the outside world that it had succeeded in re-legitimating itself in impressive fashion.[20] Inflated turnout figures were also the inevitable consequence of the ruling party's most commonly used method of committing vote fraud—simply adding votes to the PRI column. Even in the 1994 election, such "over-voting" was not entirely absent; the PAN found 936 precincts (about 1 percent of the total) in which reported voter turnout exceeded 100 percent of the registered voters. But taking the 1988 turnout figure as a fairly credible benchmark, we can have confidence that what has occurred since then represents a sharp and real increase in electoral participation.

How can we explain this participation explosion? Results from various preelection and exit polls in 1994 suggest that two key factors were responsible. First and foremost was the new, fraud-resistant electoral system installed in 1993–1994. Citizens were

[20]See José Antonio Crespo, *Urnas de Pandora: partidos políticos y elecciones en el gobierno de Salinas* (México, D.F.: CIDE-Espasa Calpe, 1995), pp. 157–58.

drawn to the polls by the novelty of an election in which, for the first time, they perceived a better-than-even chance that their vote could actually matter—that it would be respected by the government. Prospective voters trusted the process created by professionals in the newly reconstituted Federal Electoral Institute sufficiently to overcome their usual expectations of fraud. Second, there was a perception that the ruling party was actually vulnerable to defeat, a perception powerfully reinforced by the dismal performance of the PRI's Ernesto Zedillo in the first-ever, face-to-face, nationally televised debate among presidential contenders. The ruling party's perceived vulnerability motivated both PRI and opposition party sympathizers to go to the polls. As long as electoral politics remain as competitive as they have been since 1988, and potential voters continue to believe in the security of the electoral system (disregarding, at least for the moment, persisting inequities in the terms of interparty competition), we can expect further, gradual movement toward a genuinely participatory political culture in Mexico.

Government Performance

ECONOMIC GROWTH AND INEQUALITY

There is little debate about the importance of the state's contribution to the economic development of Mexico since 1940. Massive public investments in infrastructure (roads, dams, telecommunications, electrification) and generous, cheap credit provided to the private sector by Nacional Financiera and other government development banks made possible a higher rate of capital accumulation, stimulated higher levels of investment by domestic entrepreneurs and foreign corporations, and enabled Mexico to develop a diversified production capacity second only within Latin America to that of Brazil.

From 1940 until well into the 1970s, a strong elite consensus prevailed on the state's role in the economy. The state facilitated private capital accumulation and protected the capitalist system by limiting popular demands for consumption and redistribution of wealth; it established the rules for development; and it participated in the development process as the nation's largest single entrepreneur, employer, and source of investment capital. The state served as the *"rector"* (guiding force) of this mixed economy, setting broad priorities and channeling investment (both public and private) into strategic sectors. Acting through joint ventures between private firms and state-owned enterprises, the government provided resources for development projects so large that they would have been difficult or impossible to finance from internal (within-the-firm) sources or through borrowing from private banks.

The result, from the mid-1960s to the mid-1970s, was the much-touted "Mexican miracle" of sustained economic growth at annual rates of 6 to 7 percent, coupled with low inflation (5 percent per annum in the 1955–1972 period). By 1980, GNP had reached $2,130 per capita, placing Mexico toward the upper end of the World Bank's list of semi-industrialized or "middle-developed" countries.

As sole proprietor of PEMEX, the state oil monopoly, the government was responsible for developing the crucial oil and natural gas sector of the economy, which by the end of the oil boom (1978–1981) was generating more than $15 billion a year in export revenues and fueling economic growth of more than 8 percent per year—one of the world's highest growth rates.

It is the distributive consequences of this impressive performance in economic development and the manner in which it was financed by the government since the 1970s that have been criticized in retrospect. From Miguel Alemán (1946–1952) to the present, all but one or two of Mexico's presidents and their administrations embraced the private sector's contention that Mexico must first create wealth, and then worry about redistributing it; otherwise, the state would quickly be overwhelmed by popular demands that it could not satisfy. By the early 1970s, however, there was convincing evidence that an excessively large portion of Mexico's population was being left behind in the drive to become a modern, industrialized nation.

This is not to say that some benefits of the development process did not trickle down to the poor. From 1950 to 1980, poverty in absolute terms declined. The middle class expanded to an estimated 29 percent of the population by 1970. From 1960 to 1980 illiteracy dropped from 35 to 15 percent of the population, infant mortality was reduced from 78 to 70 per 1,000 live births, and average life expectancy rose from 55 to 64 years. Clearly, the quality of life for many Mexicans—even in isolated rural areas—did improve during this period, although several other Latin American countries (Chile, Colombia, Costa Rica, Cuba, Ecuador, El Salvador, and Venezuela) achieved higher rates of improvement on indicators of social well-being than did Mexico during the same period.

There was, however, a dark side to Mexico's "economic miracle." From 1950 to the mid-1970s, ownership of land and capital (stocks, bonds, time deposits) became increasingly concentrated. Personal income inequality also increased, at a time when, given Mexico's middle level of development, the national income distribution should have been shifting toward greater equality, according to classical economic development theory. Indeed, Mexico appears to have had a higher overall concentration of income in the mid-1970s than it had in 1910, before the outbreak of the revolution.[1] By 1977 the poorest 70 percent of Mexican families received

---

[1]David Felix, "Income Distribution Trends in Mexico and the Kuznets Curve," in Sylvia A. Hewlett and Richard S. Weinert, eds., *Brazil and Mexico: Patterns in Late Development* (Philadelphia: Institute for the Study of Human Issues, 1982), pp. 265–316.

only 24 percent of all disposable income, while the richest 30 percent of families received 76 percent of income. Survey data collected by INEGI, the government's statistical research agency, suggest that the country's income distribution became slightly more equal between 1977 and 1984, but this may have been due to the extraordinarily large number of new jobs created during the oil boom years of 1978–1981, most of which were eliminated during the severe economic contraction of 1982–1988. In any case, the long-term trend toward a higher degree of income inequality soon reasserted itself. Inequality increased by 10 percent between 1984 and 1989, before leveling off during the 1989–1992 period.[2]

Other social indicators mirror the trend in personal income distribution. By 1989 more than one-quarter of Mexican children under five years of age in rural areas were malnourished; the incidence of severe malnutrition among such children had risen by 100 percent during the preceding ten years.[3] While 78 percent of Mexico's elementary school-age children were enrolled in 1990, only 54 percent of those who start primary school finish it.[4] Among the dwellings included in the 1990 census, 57 percent had no sewerage connections, 50 percent had no piped water inside the dwelling, and 13 percent had no electricity.

On every indicator of economic opportunity and social well-being, there are vast disparities among Mexico's regions and between rural and urban areas. Unemployment and underemployment are concentrated overwhelmingly in the rural sector, which contains at least 70 percent of the population classified by the government as living in extreme poverty. The rate of infant mortality in rural areas is nearly 50 percent higher than the national average. Interregional disparities in social well-being are equally extreme. In 1990, the percentage of persons with incomes lower than two minimum salaries (a bare subsistence level) ranged from 40 percent in Baja California to 80 percent in Chiapas.[5] A composite index of social well-being in 1990 shows the Federal

[2]Fernando Cortés and Rosa María Rubalcava, "Equidad vía reducción: la distribución del ingreso en México, 1977–1984," unpublished paper, June 1990; Cortés and Rubalcava, "Cambio estructural y concentración: un análisis de la distribución del ingreso familiar en México, 1984–1989," paper presented at the University of Texas at Austin, April 1992; and José Córdoba, "Mexico," in John Williamson, ed., *The Political Economy of Policy Reform* (Washington, D.C.: Institute for International Economics, 1994), p. 272.

[3]Data from surveys conducted in 1979 and 1989 by the National Institute of Nutrition, reported in *Este País* 41 (August 1994), p. 40.

[4]Ministry of Education statistics analyzed by the Mexican Center for Child Resources (CEMDIN), as reported in InterPress Service (PeaceNet), "Millions of Children Out of School Despite Laws," May 27, 1994.

[5]Data compiled by the National Population Council (CONAPO), as reported in "La pobreza en México," *Este País* 40 (July 1994), p. 54.

FIGURE 4

LEVELS OF SOCIAL WELL-BEING IN 1990, BY STATE

Source: Data from INEGI, reported in Alberto Díaz Cayeros, *Desarrollo económico e inequidad regional* (México, D.F.: CIDAC-Miguel Angel Porrúa, 1995), table 3, p. 58.

District (Mexico City) and the northern border states as being the most privileged, and the southern states (especially Chiapas, Oaxaca, and Guerrero) as the most marginalized (see figure 4). Gross domestic product per capita in the same year ranged from $1,227 in Oaxaca to $8,129 in the Federal District.[6] This pattern of extreme spatial inequalities has remained essentially unchanged for several decades.

The policies and investment preferences of Mexico's post-revolutionary governments contributed much to the country's highly inegalitarian development. At minimum, the public policies pursued since 1940 failed to counteract the wealth-concentrating effects of private market forces. Evidence is strong that some government investments and policies actually reinforced these effects. For example, during most of the post-1940 period, government tax and credit policies have worked primarily to the advantage of the country's wealthiest agribusiness and industrial entrepreneurs.[7] Government expenditures for social security, public health, and education remained relatively low by international standards. By the late 1970s Mexico was still allocating a smaller share of its central government budget to social services than countries like Bolivia, Brazil, Chile, and Panama. The slowness with which basic social services were extended to the bulk of the population in Mexico was a direct consequence of the government's policy of keeping inflation low by concentrating public expenditures on subsidies and infrastructure for private industry, rather than on social programs and subsidies to consumers.

Even during the period 1970–1982, when populist policies were allegedly in vogue and government revenues were expanding rapidly because of the oil export boom, public spending for programs like health and social security remained roughly constant, in real per capita terms.[8] The economic crisis that erupted in 1982, after an unprecedented run-up in Mexico's domestic and externally held debt, made it impossible to maintain even that level of government commitment to social well-being. By 1986, debt service was consuming over half of the total federal government budget, necessitating deep cuts in spending for health, education, consumer subsidies, and job-creating public investments. Social

---

[6] Alberto Díaz Cayeros, *Desarrollo económico e inequidad regional: hacia un nuevo pacto federal en México* (México, D.F.: Miguel Angel Porrúa, CIDAC, and Fundación Friedrich Naumann, 1995), table 3, p. 58.

[7] See Carlos Elizondo, "In Search of Revenue: Tax Reform in Mexico under the Administrations of Echeverría and Salinas," *Journal of Latin American Studies* 26 (1994), pp. 159–90.

[8] Peter Ward, *Welfare Politics in Mexico: Papering Over the Cracks* (London: Allen & Unwin, 1986), pp. 9–10, 135–36.

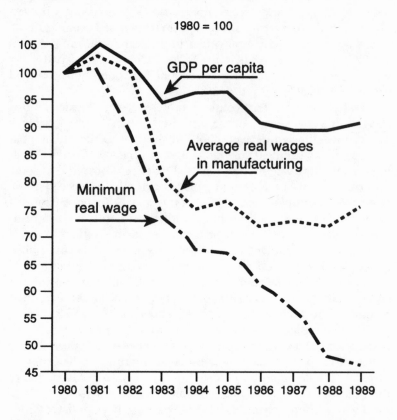

FIGURE 5

CHANGES IN GROSS DOMESTIC PRODUCT PER CAPITA, AVERAGE
REAL WAGES IN MANUFACTURING, AND MINIMUM REAL WAGES
IN URBAN EMPLOYMENT IN MEXICO, 1980–1989

Source: John Sheahan, *Conflict and Change in Mexican Economic Strategy* (La
Jolla: Center for U.S.-Mexican Studies, University of California, San Diego,
1991), p. 11.

welfare expenditures per capita fell to 1974 levels. Mexico's macroeconomic adjustment program was considerably more severe than
those in other major Latin American countries that also experienced debt crises during the 1980s.[9] The severity of the adjustment
is reflected particularly in minimum real wages, which fell by 66
percent between 1980 and 1989 (see figure 5). Despite a modest
resurgence of economic growth in the early 1990s, by the end of the

[9]See John Sheahan, *Conflict and Change in Mexican Economic Strategy: Implications for
Mexico and for Latin America* (La Jolla: Center for U.S.-Mexican Studies, University of
California, San Diego, 1991), table 2, p. 10.

Salinas *sexenio* in 1994 real wages for most Mexicans had still not recovered their levels of 1981.

Under Mexico's three most recent presidents the government has implemented a neoliberal economic development model that stresses the need to give much freer rein to market forces, both domestic and international. The strategy of import-substituting industrialization (ISI), which the Mexican government pursued from the 1940s through the 1970s, had stressed the development of domestic industry and an internal market for its products, through an elaborate set of incentives to consumers (relatively high real wages and generous benefits, at least to unionized workers) and producers (for example, tariff protection from imports). In contrast, the post-1982 development model sought to create an open,more efficient, globally competitive economy in which Mexico's exports, rather than expansion of the domestic consumer market, would become the driving force. Among other fundamental changes, the implementation of this model required a tight wage policy (meaning that, at least temporarily, real wages must fall), drastic shrinking of the public sector of the economy through a sweeping privatization program, and opening up nearly all sectors to private investment (including those formerly reserved to the state). Through this so-called technocratic free-market revolution, Mexico would create a more attractive investment climate (especially for foreign capital) and push up its rate of economic growth.

While striving to unleash market forces, the technocrats who dominated economic policy making in the post-1982 period were unwilling to completely surrender the government's traditional "rectorship" role in the economy. "The model was Taiwan or South Korea, not [Milton] Friedman Chile. The new [government] elite did not believe that the market, left to its own devices, would resolve all problems through invisible hands."[10]

This concern is reflected in the Salinas administration's considerable spending on social welfare programs like National Solidarity—an explicit effort to construct a minimal safety net for the millions of low-income Mexicans who would inevitably be among the short-term "losers" from market-oriented economic policies and trade liberalization under NAFTA. Unfortunately, these carefully targeted social programs have not been sufficient to offset the structural impoverishment caused by falling real wages, the elimination of millions of jobs, and the slashing of most consumer subsidies.

---

[10]Centeno, *Democracy within Reason*, p. 194.

A controversial national survey conducted jointly by a United Nations agency and the Mexican government in 1992 found 37.2 million Mexicans (43.8 percent of the total population) living at or below the official poverty line.[11] An independent, academic study using official and private-sector statistics found that from 1963 to 1981, before the shift to neoliberal economic policies, the proportion of Mexico's population living below the poverty line had dropped from 77.5 to 48.5 percent; however, from 1982 to 1992, the trend was reversed, with the poverty population rising to 66 percent.[12]

Whatever statistical base is used, it is clear that the new, market-oriented development model thus far has exacerbated— not alleviated—Mexico's poverty and inequality problems, even when the model was apparently working well in macroeconomic terms (that is, from 1989 through 1992).[13] Moreover, Mexico's experience with rapid economic growth during the "miracle" years of the 1950s and 1960s and the oil boom of the late 1970s and early 1980s suggests that without strong, sustained government action to correct for market failures and improve human capital endowments through education and job training, income concentration and related social problems will continue unabated.

In the aftermath of the economic collapse of 1994–1995, even technocrats in President Zedillo's cabinet were suggesting that full recovery might require a (partial?) return to the long-discredited ISI strategy, in order to boost domestic consumption.[14] While a total scrapping of the neoliberal model seems unlikely and unrealistic at this historical juncture, the most recent economic shocks have raised new concerns about the costs and benefits of that model. A new debate over national development options has been ignited.

---

[11] United Nations/CEPAL and INEGI, "Informe sobre la magnitud y evolución de la pobreza en México, 1984–1992," unpublished report, Mexico City, October 24, 1993.

[12] Eduardo Hernández and Julio Boltvinik, "Informe sobre la pobreza en México," Universidad Autónoma de México and El Colegio de México, Mexico City, April 1995. The December 1994 devaluation and the sharp rise in inflation (to 45–50 percent in 1995) that accompanied it caused such a massive loss of purchasing power that another 14 percent of Mexicans may have been pushed below the poverty line, according to initial estimates ("Markets Not Convinced by Official Optimism," *Mexico and NAFTA Report*, p. 7).

[13] An apparent reduction in *extreme* poverty at the national level during this period, documented by official surveys conducted in 1989 and 1992 (see Córdoba, "Mexico," p. 271), masks a significant increase in the absolute number of "extremely poor" Mexicans residing in rural areas during the same years. See Wayne A. Cornelius, "Designing Social Policy for Mexico's Liberalized Economy: From Social Services and Infrastructure to Job Creation," in Riordan Roett, ed., *The Challenges of Institutional Reform in Mexico* (Boulder, Colo.: Lynne Rienner, 1995), pp. 139–53.

[14] Fred Rosen, "Pacts and Debates," *El Financiero International*, October 30–November 5, 1995, p. 2.

CONTROLLING POPULATION GROWTH AND CREATING JOBS

From the early nineteenth century through the 1930s, the Mexican population expanded at a relatively moderate rate. Around 1940 it began a sharp upward climb, as advances in public health reduced the mortality rate while the birthrate remained constant. The population grew from 20 million in 1940 to 35 million in 1960 to at least 81 million in 1990.[15] By the early 1970s Mexico's rate of population growth had reached 3.5 percent per year—one of the world's highest growth rates.

In 1973 President Luis Echeverría was convinced by his advisers that the huge resources that would be needed to feed, educate, and provide productive employment for a population doubling in size every 20 years were beyond Mexico's possibilities. A nationwide family planning program was launched in 1974, and within a few years the birthrate had begun to fall noticeably. The average number of children born to each woman dropped from 6.8 in 1970 to under 3 in 1994. By 1995 Mexico had a population estimated at 93 million, growing at a rate of slightly less than 2 percent per year. Consequently, instead of having a population of 130 million by the year 2000 (as projected in the mid-1970s), Mexico is expected to enter the new millennium with some 106 million inhabitants.[16]

Regardless of Mexico's recent success in limiting new births, the country's labor force is still growing by about 3.5 percent annually because of the high birthrates of the 1960s and early 1970s. This growth rate adds about 1 million persons to the ranks of job seekers every year. Unfortunately, since 1982 very rapid labor force growth in Mexico has coincided with a period of stagnation in job creation. By 1986 open unemployment had risen to an estimated 15.4 percent. The official unemployment rate fell below 6 percent in 1990, as the recovery from the economic crisis of the 1980s gained momentum. But both of these statistics greatly understate the magnitude of Mexico's employment problem. The government considers a person employed if he or she works only one hour per week, and World Bank studies suggest that *under*employment is a far more significant problem than open unemployment, affecting perhaps 25 to 35 percent of the economically active population.[17]

---

[15]The official census count was 81.1 million inhabitants, but this figure may reflect significant undercounting. Demographers have estimated that the true population size in 1990 was about 84.9 million.

[16]Víctor L. Urquidi, "Algunas lecciones para la política mexicana de población," *Carta sobre Población* (newsletter of the Grupo Académico de Apoyo a Programas de Población, México, D.F.) 2:5 (January 1995), p. 2.

[17]World Bank, *Mexico after the Oil Boom: Refashioning a Development Strategy* (Washington, D.C., June 1987).

Many of these underemployed Mexicans, as well as first-time job seekers and those whose jobs have been eliminated by economic restructuring and liberalized foreign trade, have taken refuge in the so-called informal economy, working as unlicensed street vendors, washing windshields at busy intersections, sewing garments in their homes, and performing a wide variety of other tasks outside of the "formal" sector. This underground economy employs an estimated 24 to 45 percent of Mexico's total work force, depending on different definitions and methodological assumptions.[18] A significant portion of Mexico's unemployment and underemployment is also exported to the United States, via illegal immigration.

Perhaps the greatest deficiency of Mexico's post-1940 development strategy has been the failure to develop an employment base adequate to absorb the labor force growth of the 1980s and 1990s. In the countryside, massive government investments in irrigation projects, "green revolution" technologies, infrastructure, and agricultural credit programs all benefited large producers far more than small farmers. This placed even greater capital resources in the hands of large landowners, who were able to mechanize their operations more rapidly. In agriculture as well as urban-based industry, government subsidies for acquisition of labor-saving machinery made it financially attractive for large producers to substitute capital for labor.

Econometric modeling studies indicate that during the 15 years between 1985 and 1999, Mexico will have added only 881,000 formal-sector jobs, while the number of new job seekers during the same period will reach 17.1 million. Not included in this figure are the estimated 2.3 million Mexicans who were jobless in 1985 ("accumulated unemployment"). The same studies project that between 1985 and 1999, employment in the formal sector of the economy will have fallen from 83.4 percent of the work force to 52.6 percent, while employment in the informal sector mushroomed.[19]

Such alarming projections are consistent with the actual track record of job creation in Mexico from 1980 through 1994. Net job creation has been anemic, despite a huge influx of foreign capital from 1989 to 1994. This dismal performance can be explained in part by the fact that well over half of the foreign funds received by

[18]See, for example, Centro de Estudios Económicos del Sector Privado, *La economía subterránea en México* (México, D.F.: Editorial Diana, 1987); and Bryan R. Roberts, "The Dynamics of Informal Employment in Mexico," in U.S. Dept. of Labor, Bureau of International Affairs, *Work without Protections: Case Studies of the Informal Sector in Developing Countries* (Washington, D.C., 1993), pp. 101–25.

[19]Estimates from Wharton School of Business Econometrics, reported in Carlos Ramírez, "The Fourth World," *El Financiero International,* April 17, 1995.

Mexico during this period were being invested in stocks, short-term government-issued bonds, and other financial instruments, rather than in job-creating direct investment projects. Equally important, the government's strategy of promoting export-led development has induced many private firms to become more competitive in the global marketplace by shedding labor and becoming more capital intensive. For example, the aggregate work force of Mexico's 500 most important exporting companies fell by 2.6 percent between 1992 and 1993.[20] The proportion of Mexicans working in manufacturing industry has fallen each year since 1988, and manufacturing employment (excluding the *maquiladora* in-bond assembly sector) actually declined in absolute terms by up to 400,000 jobs during the Salinas *sexenio*.[21]

Thus, it has yet to be proven that economic liberalization and free trade can yield significantly higher rates of economic growth and job creation, especially in Mexico's small and medium-sized businesses, only about 12 percent of which export anything.[22] The character of economic development being generated in Mexico by the neoliberal model seems incompatible with the country's overwhelming social requirements. There is a growing consensus that the government will have to do much more to upgrade workers' skills through vocational education and subsidized, on-the-job training, if Mexico is to realize a greater return from its painful shift to an open, market-oriented development strategy.

FINANCING DEVELOPMENT AND CONTROLLING INFLATION

From 1940 to 1970 Mexico's public sector acquired an international reputation for sound, conservative monetary and fiscal policies. This conservative style of economic management, coupled with

[20]National survey of firms commissioned by *Expansión* magazine, Mexico City, 1994.

[21]See Enrique Dussel Peters, "From Export-Oriented to Import-Oriented Industrialization: Recent Developments in Mexico's Manufacturing Sector, 1988–1994," in Gerardo Otero, ed., *Neoliberal Revolution: Economic Restructuring and Politics in Mexico* (Boulder, Colo.: Westview, forthcoming).

[22]Calculated from the survey data presented in Clemente Ruiz Durán and Carlos Zubirán Schadtler, *Cambios en la estructura industrial y el papel de las micro, pequeñas y medianas empresas en México* (México, D.F.: Nacional Financiera, 1992), p. 158. Contributing to the dilemma of small and medium-sized firms is the highly oligopolistic nature of the Mexican economy, which neoliberal policies appear to have reinforced. As a U.S.-based investment banker recently observed, "If we look at beverages, cement, media, banking, and other sectors [of the Mexican economy] we find a lot of concentration. You have a large universe of small and medium companies that have to compete with very large companies that have access to international capital and . . . international levels of technology. The small and medium-sized companies semi-survive in a highly disadvantageous environment." (Jorge Mariscal, Vice President, Goldman Sach; quoted in *El Financiero International*, October 30–November 5, 1995, p. 8.)

Mexico's long record of political stability, gave the country an attractive investment climate. By 1982 this image had been shattered; the public sector (and much of the private sector) was suffering from a deep liquidity crisis, and inflation had reached levels unheard of since the first decade of the Mexican Revolution, when paper currencies lost most of their value. What happened?

The basic difficulty was that the government had attempted to spend its way out of the social and economic problems that had accumulated since 1940, without paying the political cost that sweeping redistributive policies would have entailed. Instead, it attempted to expand the entire economic pie by enlarging the state's role as banker, entrepreneur, and employer. Throughout the period since 1940, and especially after 1970, Mexico's public sector expanded steadily while its revenue-raising capability lagged. The result was ever-larger government deficits, financed increasingly by borrowing abroad.

For most of the post–World War II period, Mexico's tax effort—its rate of taxation and its actual performance in collecting taxes—was among the poorest in the world. Officials feared that any major alteration in the tax structure would stampede domestic and foreign capital out of the country. Two modest attempts at tax reform, in 1964 and 1972, failed because of determined opposition from the business community. When the private sector refused to accede to higher taxes, the Echeverría administration opted for large-scale deficit financing, external indebtedness, and a huge increase in the money supply. The public sector itself was vastly enlarged as the number of state-owned enterprises increased from 84 in 1970 to 845 in 1976. Fiscal restraint was finally forced on the government by depletion of its currency reserves in 1976.

Echeverría's successor, José López Portillo, at first attempted to reverse the trend toward larger government deficits, but the effort was abandoned when the treasury began to swell with oil export revenues. Again, the temptation was to address basic structural problems by further expanding the state sector, and López Portillo found it impossible to resist. Oil revenues seemed to be a guaranteed, limitless source of income for the government. Mexico borrowed heavily abroad, anticipating a steady rise in oil prices.

Although Mexico's long-term foreign debt (owed by both the government and private Mexican firms) had grown substantially during the Echeverría *sexenio* (from $12.1 billion in 1970 to $30.5 billion in 1976), the most rapid expansion occurred during López Portillo's oil boom administration. By the end of 1982 Mexico's external debt totaled nearly $82 billion, with annual interest payments of $16 billion (compared with $475 million paid to service the debt in 1970). In August 1982 the government was forced to suspend repayment of principal and begin a difficult renegotiation of the size and terms of the debt with Mexico's foreign creditors—the first of several such "restructurings," the most recent of which was completed in 1990. By 1994, Mexico had reduced its total long-term external debt to about 40 percent of gross domestic product (compared with nearly 60 percent in 1987), but in absolute terms the external debt was higher than ever, exceeding $120 billion, and annual interest payments still consumed about 15 percent of the country's export earnings.[23]

Deficit financing, especially in the context of the overheated economy of the oil boom years, also touched off a burst of inflation. The average annual inflation rate rose from 15 percent during Echeverría's presidency (nearly triple the average rate during the 1940–1970 period) to 36 percent under López Portillo and 91 percent in the de la Madrid *sexenio* (159 percent in 1987). Both the de la Madrid and Salinas administrations made reducing the inflation rate their top economic priority, but Salinas was much more effective in bringing inflation under control than his predecessor. His principal instrument was price and wage controls, enforced by a formal, government–business–organized labor "pact" that was renewed six times, with some adjustments, at 12- to 18-month intervals. This form of shock therapy brought the inflation rate down to single digits by 1994.

The other key to Salinas's success in fighting inflation was deep cuts in spending to reduce and eventually eliminate the public deficit, coupled with unprecedented steps to boost federal government revenues. These measures included the selling or closure of hundreds of state-owned enterprises, vigorous enforcement of the tax laws (only two individual tax evaders had been caught and imprisoned between 1921 and 1988), and the introduction of a 2 percent annual tax on total business assets, intended to reduce manipulations that had previously enabled 70 percent of Mexico's businesses to evade paying any taxes.

Even after the Salinas administration's "successful" tax reform, however, the federal government still obtained most of its revenues (over 60 percent) from socially regressive indirect taxes, primarily the IVA (value-added tax) levied on about 70 percent of all goods and services. Personal income tax rates for the wealthiest Mexicans were actually reduced from 50 percent in 1988 to 35 percent in 1990, and a proposed tax on capital gains by individual investors in the stock market was shelved. "As on previous occasions, the government decided it was too risky to tax the savings of the richest

[23]Inter-American Development Bank, *Latin America in Graphs: Demographic, Economic, and Social Trends, 1994–1995* (Baltimore, Md.: Johns Hopkins University Press, 1995), p. 192.

Mexicans. The threat of capital flight . . . remained a powerful constraint on the government's taxing powers."[24]

The deep financial crisis that erupted in the first month of Ernesto Zedillo's presidency raised serious questions about the wisdom of the Salinas administration's obsessive pursuit of one-digit inflation, as well as its decision to "live with" a seriously overvalued peso until after the August 1994 national elections—indeed, until after President Salinas had left office. An earlier, staged devaluation would have boosted inflation and interest rates at a politically inopportune moment; but it could have prevented the financial panic, massive capital flight, and even higher inflation that followed the sudden mega-devaluation of December 20, 1994. Inflation in 1995 was expected to exceed 50 percent, as compared with 7 percent in the preceding year.

Salinas and his financial ministers were also justly criticized for creating illusions of prosperity by financing a huge current accounts deficit (resulting mostly from a flood of consumer imports) with short-term, highly speculative capital. That "hot money"—mostly from large, U.S. institutional investors—flowed into *tesobonos*, the high-yielding, U.S. dollar–denominated bonds with maturities ranging from 28 to 180 days that were issued by the Mexican Treasury in prodigious quantities beginning in 1989. By the end of 1994, Mexico's debt in *tesobonos* had grown to almost $30 billion, and with the central bank's reserves virtually depleted by its efforts to fend off six speculative attacks on the peso during 1994, there was no way to pay off these bonds as they matured. Only a massive international "bailout" could avoid default, the imposition of currency controls (to prevent further capital flight), and a general economic meltdown.

How could a technocratic government that had earned worldwide respect for its skillful management of the economy, even in the midst of the political shocks of 1994, have erred so grievously? There is, as yet, no definitive explanation. Most likely, the debacle resulted from a combination of personal and political considerations on Salinas's part (for example, the need to paper over the financial cracks that were developing in order to achieve a decisive PRI victory in the August 21 national elections; a desire to protect his image in the midst of a difficult and ultimately unsuccessful campaign to become head of the newly established World Trade Organization after he left the presidency), strong resistance by Salinas's treasury secretary, Pedro Aspe, to an abrupt devaluation, and the ineptitude and inexperience of Zedillo's economic team in dealing with skittish private foreign investors. Salinas and his

---

[24]Elizondo, "In Search of Revenue," p. 179.

economic cabinet could also have assumed that drastic adjustments in 1994 were unnecessary. Indeed, the official story, as articulated by Salinas's former chief of staff, is that "he thought the [financial] imbalances and pressures had political origins and that once the elections were over and there was a peaceful transition, confidence would come back."[25]

Whatever the truth, the Mexican government has suffered a severe loss of credibility, at home and abroad, and rebuilding confidence in its economic management capabilities will require years of effort. Meanwhile, Mexico will have to finance a much larger portion of its economic growth from domestic savings. Raising the domestic savings rate (in 1994, about 16 to 17 percent; at least 25 percent is needed to meet long-term investment needs) looms as one of the greatest structural challenges facing Mexico's economic policy makers. Responding to the magnitude and urgency of this challenge, the Zedillo government in late 1995 moved to restructure the social security system, encouraging workers to open individual retirement accounts that would offer higher rates of return and attract more savings.

---

[25]José Córdoba Montoya, quoted in *El Financiero International*, April 17–23, 1995, p. 2.

Mexico's Political Future:
Transition to What?

> The obvious truth about Mexico . . .
> is that one system is falling apart on us,
> but we have no other system to put in its place.
> —*Carlos Fuentes*[1]

It is widely believed today that the Mexican political system, as we
have known it since 1940, is in an advanced state of decomposition.
In 1994, with elections operating under strict new, fraud-resistant
rules and the government no longer controlling the certification of
results, Mexicans had their first real chance to end the PRI's long
reign in power at the national level, but only about half could bring
themselves to actually take that chance. The opposition vote was
so fragmented that a plurality victory by the PRI was inevitable.

With the economic collapse of 1994–1995 and the still-unfold-
ing political scandals over high-profile assassinations, drug traffic
protection schemes, and corrupt business dealings within the
PRIista elite, most Mexicans feel exasperated and betrayed. In a
poll of Mexico City residents conducted just six months after the
elections, only 20 percent of the respondents said that they would
vote again for the PRI if new elections were to be held today; the
remainder of those expressing a preference would divide their
votes among the PAN (25 percent), the PRD (25 percent), and other
smaller opposition parties (7 percent). On the other hand, only 32
percent of the interviewees in the same survey preferred that the
PRI "disappear" as a political party (the majority wished that it
would reform itself drastically), and nearly two-thirds believed
that if another party were in power, the same economic problems

---

[1] Carlos Fuentes, *Christopher Unborn* (New York: Farrar, Strauss, Giroux, 1989).

would be afflicting the country.[2] Here, in a nutshell, is the dilemma and the opportunity confronting would-be political reformers in Mexico today.

The accelerated breakdown of the one-party-dominant system in Mexico urgently raises the question of what will replace it. Most Mexicans—even many members of the ruling political elite—are highly skeptical that the PRI is reformable. They doubt that it can be transformed into a real political party, capable of competing successfully, on its own, in the much more competitive electoral environment that has developed in Mexico since the 1980s. However, many Mexicans also see the two main opposition parties as having serious liabilities and limitations, and fear that they may not be ready to govern at the national level.

Mexico has emerged from the last seven years of political turmoil with a de facto three-party system, in which we can reasonably anticipate that the PAN and, to a much lesser degree, the PRD will continue to build on their gains in 1994, especially if they can effectively exploit their expanded presence in both houses of the federal Congress and President Zedillo's commitment to a more equal balance of executive and legislative powers. Under Mexico's partial proportional representation system, a relatively small shift in the vote distribution could lead to a large reshuffling of seats in the Congress. The result could be a divided government, as early as the midterm elections of 1997.

At the state and local levels, vigorously competitive *two*-party systems are emerging faster than anyone anticipated a decade ago. The probable result will be more governorships won by the opposition parties, which should help them build their credibility as alternatives to PRI governance and raise the visibility and presidential prospects of some of their leaders. In light of developments since 1988, especially the electoral successes of the PAN and the disappointments of the PRD, it seems more likely that nationally viable opposition parties will emerge from their regional bases of strength, rather than be constructed from above by national-level leaders. An additional consequence of more intense electoral competition in subnational political spaces should be a reinvigoration of federalism in Mexico, as both opposition-controlled and PRIista state governments strive to launch their own initiatives, rather than simply implement or react to central government directives. Moreover, if Zedillo gives his party complete autonomy in the selection of its candidates, this may expedite the emergence

---

[2]Rafael Giménez, "Creen que PRI debe tener cambios fuertes," *Reforma* (México, D.F.), March 4, 1995, p. 1. The poll was conducted on March 2 and 3, 1995. The margin of sampling error is plus or minus 4.4 percentage points.

of the kind of energetic, new-style PRI leaders that presidential impositions have systematically discouraged.

Whether decentralization, executive-legislative power sharing, and a continuation of the high level of mass political participation witnessed in recent elections will be enough to move Mexico irrevocably into an orderly transition to Western-style democracy is impossible to predict at this juncture. Much will depend on the kind of role that President Zedillo chooses to play in managing the transition. Two, quite different scenarios are plausible.

In the most optimistic of these scenarios, Zedillo will continue to play the role of enlightened reformer, vigorously overhauling the judicial system (both to placate strong domestic demands and to convince foreign investors that their property rights and contracts in Mexico will be protected by an impartial, efficient legal system[3]); equalizing the terms of electoral competition by dissolving PRI-government symbiosis and pushing another set of electoral system reforms through the Congress to help level the playing field in the areas of campaign finance and media access; allowing his PANista attorney general to pursue his investigations of the mega-political homicides of 1993–1994 to their ultimate conclusions and letting the chips fall where they may. By demonstrating his competence and conviction as a political reformer, Zedillo will enhance popular support for his presidency and make it easier for the opposition parties to collaborate with him on a variety of issues. If it becomes necessary to discipline members of his own party in the Congress or the state governments who are resisting his reforms, Zedillo will not shirk from using the traditional powers of the presidency to do so.

Indeed, the critical ingredient of success in this scenario is the maintenance of strong presidential rule during a difficult period of transition. The conventional wisdom among Mexican political analysts, until quite recently, has been that *limiting* presidential power—not preserving it in the hope that it will be used for laudable ends—is the necessary, if not sufficient, condition for democratization in Mexico.[4] Revisionist thinking recognizes that "a weakened presidency in a context with so many antidemocratic pressures actually reduces prospects for reform," and that the president must be able to negotiate with the opponents of democratization from a position of strength.[5]

---

[3]On the importance of judicial system reform to Mexico's future economic growth, see Luis Rubio, "The Rule of Law and Development," in Klaus Schwab, ed., *Overcoming Indifference: Ten Key Challenges in Today's Changing World* (New York: New York University Press, 1995), chap. 10.

[4]See, for example, Meyer, "Democratization of the PRI: Mission Impossible?"

[5]Personal communication from John Bailey, March 12, 1995.

The pessimistic scenario for political change in Mexico during the next five years assumes the persistence of dangerous power vacuums that President Zedillo will be either unwilling or unable to fill. With the president refusing to play his traditional role as head of the PRI, the ruling elite will be torn asunder, as hard-line "dinosaurs" and would-be reformers within the party are left to fight it out among themselves for nominations to elective office. The national-level PRI may implode, leaving large portions of the country under the control of 1920s-style political warlords. If real power is dispersed to the thousands of local *caciques*, state-level *caudillos*, and national-level power brokers who have long been the backbone of the PRI-government apparatus, it may become impossible for Zedillo to accomplish his aims. Rather than a rejuvenated, reformist PRI leadership at state and local levels, there would be a stronger alliance among old-guard politicians aimed at preserving the machinery of authoritarian control and protecting their personal financial interests. And if the PRI loses majority control of the Congress in the 1997 midterm elections, another crucial lever of presidential control will be eliminated. Less and less encumbered by presidential authority, intra-elite conflict may produce a series of political impasses to which the regime may be unable to respond effectively. The few rules of the traditional system that have not yet been broken by either Salinas or Zedillo could safely be ignored by other political actors.

Perhaps the most benign outcome of this scenario would be temporary paralysis in politics and policy making, followed by a nonviolent reconfiguration of the party system. Either the "dinosaurs" will triumph in the struggle for control of the PRI, or the party will be irrevocably split, with old-style politicians and modernizing technocrats going their own separate ways, taking whatever supporters they can muster and forming new alliances. However, if this second scenario should materialize, the Zedillo presidency could culminate in ungovernability, political cannibalism, and a highly conflicted transition to a new set of political arrangements that might be even less democratic than the present ones. Under President Zedillo, several state governors associated with the PRI's hard-line, antireform faction have openly defied various presidential initiatives and blocked efforts to reform their states' political institutions and electoral laws. The breakdown of political control and ruling party discipline at the center has made it possible for these and other state and local political actors to operate with extraordinary autonomy.

In short, we may be witnessing the fragmentation of authoritarianism in Mexico, or the emergence of a more "crisis-prone" but still essentially stable authoritarian system.[6] Of course, there is no reason to expect a hardened, deeply corrupt regime that required 66 years to be built to end quickly and smoothly, with hardly a whimper. Transitions from authoritarianism to democracy are invariably messy and conflictual; Mexico's experience will probably be no different. In any event, the tremendous political and economic shocks to the system in recent years—and especially since January 1, 1994—have created conditions favorable to a democratic breakthrough that have never before existed in post-revolutionary Mexico.

[6]See Cornelius, Gentleman, and Smith, eds., *Mexico's Alternative Political Futures*, pp. 40–41; and Dresser, "Five Scenarios for Mexico," pp. 70–71.

For Further Reading

Aitken, Robert, et al., eds. *Dismantling the Mexican State*. London: Macmillan, 1995.

Bailey, John J. *Governing Mexico: The Statecraft of Crisis Management*. New York: St. Martin's Press, 1988.

Bethell, Leslie, ed. *Mexico since Independence*. Cambridge and New York: Cambridge University Press, 1991.

Camp, Roderic A. *Entrepreneurs and Politics in Twentieth Century Mexico*. New York: Oxford University Press, 1989.

———. *Generals in the Palacio: The Military in Modern Mexico*. New York: Oxford University Press, 1992.

———. *Political Recruitment across Two Centuries: Mexico, 1884–1991*. Austin: University of Texas Press, 1995.

Carr, Barry. *Marxism and Communism in Twentieth-Century Mexico*. Lincoln: University of Nebraska Press, 1992.

Centeno, Miguel Angel. *Democracy within Reason: Technocratic Revolution in Mexico*. University Park: Pennsylvania State University Press, 1994.

Collier, George A., and Elizabeth L. Quaratiello. *Basta!—Land and the Zapatista Rebellion in Chiapas*. Oakland, Calif.: Food First Books, Institute for Food and Development Policy, 1994.

Cook, Maria L., Kevin J. Middlebrook, and Juan Molinar Horcasitas, eds. *The Politics of Economic Restructuring: State-Society Relations and Regime Change in Mexico*. La Jolla: Center for U.S.-Mexican Studies, University of California, San Diego, 1994.

Cornelius, Wayne A. *Politics and the Migrant Poor in Mexico City*. Stanford, Calif.: Stanford University Press, 1975.

Cornelius, Wayne A., Ann L. Craig, and Jonathan Fox, eds. *Transforming State-Society Relations in Mexico: The National Solidarity Strategy*. La Jolla: Center for U.S.-Mexican Studies, University of California, San Diego, 1994.

Cornelius, Wayne A., Judith Gentleman, and Peter H. Smith, eds. *Mexico's Alternative Political Futures*. La Jolla: Center for U.S.-Mexican Studies, University of California, San Diego, 1989.

Davis, Diane E. *Urban Leviathan: Mexico City in the Twentieth Century*. Philadelphia: Temple University Press, 1994.

Domínguez, Jorge I., and James A. McCann. *Democratizing Mexico: Public Opinion and Elections*. Baltimore, Md.: Johns Hopkins University Press, 1995.

Foweraker, Joe, and Ann L. Craig, eds. *Popular Movements and Political Change in Mexico*. Boulder, Colo.: Lynne Rienner, 1990.

Fox, Jonathan. *The Politics of Food in Mexico: State Power and Social Mobilization*. Ithaca, N.Y.: Cornell University Press, 1992.

Gentleman, Judith, ed. *Mexican Politics in Transition*. Boulder, Colo.: Westview, 1987.

González de la Rocha, Mercedes. *The Resources of Poverty: Women and Survival in a Mexican City*. Oxford and Cambridge, Mass.: Blackwell, 1994.

Grindle, Merilee S. *Challenging the State: Crisis and Innovation in Latin America and Africa*. New York: Cambridge University Press, 1995.

Harvey, Neil A., with Luis Hernández Navarro and Jeffrey W. Rubin. *Rebellion in Chiapas: Rural Reforms, Campesino Radicalism and the Limits to Salinismo*. La Jolla: Center for U.S.-Mexican Studies, University of California, San Diego, 1994.

Hellman, Judith Adler. *Mexican Lives*. New York: The New Press, 1994.

Joseph, Gilbert M., and Daniel Nugent, eds. *Everyday Forms of State Formation: Revolution and the Negotiation of Rule in Modern Mexico*. Durham, N.C.: Duke University Press, 1994.

Knight, Alan. *The Mexican Revolution*. 2 vols. Lincoln: University of Nebraska Press, 1990.

Lustig, Nora. *Mexico: The Remaking of an Economy*. Washington, D.C.: Brookings Institution, 1992.

Maxfield, Sylvia. *Governing Capital: International Finance and Mexican Politics*. Ithaca, N.Y.: Cornell University Press, 1990.

Middlebrook, Kevin J. *The Paradox of Revolution: Labor, the State, and Authoritarianism in Mexico*. Baltimore, Md.: Johns Hopkins University Press, 1995.

Morris, Stephen D. *Political Reformism in Mexico*. Boulder, Colo.: Lynne Rienner, 1995.

Rodríguez, Victoria E., and Peter M. Ward. *Political Change in Baja California: Democracy in the Making?* La Jolla: Center for U.S.-Mexican Studies, University of California, San Diego, 1995.

Rodríguez, Victoria E., and Peter M. Ward, eds. *Opposition Government in Mexico*. Albuquerque: University of New Mexico Press, 1995.

Rubin, Jeffrey. *Decentering the Regime: History, Culture, and Radical Politics in Juchitán, Mexico*. Durham, N.C.: Duke University Press, forthcoming 1996.

Smith, Peter H. *Labyrinths of Power: Political Recruitment in Twentieth Century Mexico*. Princeton, N.J.: Princeton University Press, 1979.

Ward, Peter M. *Welfare Politics in Mexico: Papering Over the Cracks*. London: Allen and Unwin, 1986.

About the Author

Wayne A. Cornelius is Professor of Political Science and Adjunct Professor of International Relations and Pacific Studies at the University of California, San Diego. He also holds the Gildred Chair in U.S.-Mexican Relations at the same institution. He was the founding Director (1979–1994) of the Center for U.S.-Mexican Studies and continues to serve as the Center's Director of Studies and Programs. He has conducted field research in Mexico since 1962. His most recent books include *Transforming State-Society Relations in Mexico: The National Solidarity Strategy* (coeditor, Center for U.S.-Mexican Studies, 1994), *Controlling Immigration: A Global Perspective* (coeditor/coauthor, Stanford University Press, 1995), and *California's Immigrant Children: Theory, Research, and Implications for Educational Policy* (coeditor, Center for U.S.-Mexican Studies, 1995). He is a frequent commentator on Mexican politics and development issues for the *Los Angeles Times*, the *New York Times*, and other major newspapers and newsmagazines in the United States and Mexico. His current research projects include a study of agricultural policy reform in Mexico in the 1990s, and a volume on the interface between local politics and democratization processes in Mexico and Cuba.